Sons and Daughters

This Generation and the Spirit of Adoption

DENISE BUCKBINDER GANUCHEAU

WESTBOW°
PRESS
A DIVISION OF THOMAS NELSON
& ZONDERVAN

WestBow Press books may be ordered through booksellers or by contacting:

WestBow Press
A Division of Thomas Nelson & Zondervan
1663 Liberty Drive
Bloomington, IN 47403
www.westbowpress.com
1 (866) 928-1240

Cover and author photographs by Rebekah Greenawalt.

All photographs copyright © 2013 Denise Ganucheau.

ISBN: 978-1-4908-4684-2 (sc)
ISBN: 978-1-4908-4685-9 (hc)
ISBN: 978-1-4908-4686-6 (e)

Library of Congress Control Number: 2014913727

Printed in the United States of America.

WestBow Press rev. date: 12/9/2014

Contents

Prologue

Finding The Call

In the summer of 2007, I had been fasting off and on for thirty-nine days when I made a last minute decision to take the 10 hour drive from Arlington, Texas, to Nashville, Tennessee. I trusted my friends from The Prayer Room ministry even though I hadn't known them long. The bonding point was that I had spent three to five days a week during the past six months with them, usually at five in the morning, praying for our city and our nation. We had a heartfelt tie; we were passionate about our God and about the people living in our cities. Spending hours together pouring our hearts out to the Lord was no solitary job. I heard the hearts of those in the room all around me and gained a trust towards them that one could not imagine in any other scenario, save a family of the same household. And to put it frankly, we *were* our own family. That is the best way I can describe our close--knit web of friendships. We had seen all we needed to know that we were in this together. We helped each other, encouraged each other, and often checked in on one another to make sure no one was in a place of need or want.

What I find plainly amazing is that because I had such a trust and a peace, I packed my bags and decided to see what this thing, TheCall, was all about. It was scheduled on July 7, 2007, or "7-7-07" as many people often referred to it. There was a mandate. Something was going on in the church and in the Spirit. There was a call for holiness and fasting, a call to plead for the mercy of God on our country. Lou Engle is a great man of God who founded TheCall, where thousands of young people gather to pray, fast, and seek the Lord's face on behalf of our nation. The Lord has given Lou such a burden of responsibility to see holiness arise and wicked ways abandoned in our culture, that he has dedicated his life to it. The ministry has sights set on the young generation and what potential it has for calling on the reviving power of the living God for this nation.

So with the passions of patriotism, holiness, righteousness, and love of God planted deep inside me from the time I was just a young girl, I was "called" to TheCall, even though I did not fully understand it at the time. I prayed with The Prayer Room ministry, and I fasted as much as I could with them. Lou often encouraged people not to give up but to try again if they messed up during a fast. Pastor Steve Robinson from Church of the King, often quoted John Maxwell saying "failing isn't failing; quitting is failing." So with every ounce of passion, the "fasters" pressed on. It wasn't about our performance anyway. All I knew is that my heart moved when we prayed, and it moved when I thought about the gathering with so many other believers and radical worshipers. I saw and felt the Spirit of God take root in our prayer meetings and in the messages Lou sent out. These encouraged my faith and stirred God's Spirit within me until I was relentless to see repentance and the call to holiness fulfilled. I wanted in total to see our nation move towards God and not away from Him. I had caught a glimpse of a vision, and I was hungry for more. All these things put together allowed me to hit the road with my praying friends in Christ.

It was a long drive to Nashville but an awesome bonding experience, where we learned even more about each other than before. When we finally arrived, I headed for my hotel room and met up with my female roommates. That night several of us went out in the city, where several ministry events surrounding TheCall were scheduled. I saw many worship venues and heard of multiple speaking engagements and teaching sessions that were all held in a close walking proximity. I was utterly amazed. I could walk down the street and see a hotel rocking with worship, and see kids coming and going to other events in other buildings on the same street. It was like the house was shaking for God. It was as if Christianity had taken over. Try to picture a world where it is the norm to walk down the street on a Friday night and see all kinds of Spirit-filled parties and energetic teachings. It was more like a down-town feel--alive with music and bustle, but it was all God!

Early the next morning before the main event began, what seemed like a multitude of people gathered before TheCall team and Lou Engel. We came to make a repentance walk from one location of downtown to Titan Stadium. The start of the walk was slow because there were so many people taking the repentance walk for our nation. It wasn't until my portion of the silent crowd found its way to the street that I saw a mind-blowing sight! Let me explain this to you. As far as my eye could see forward when the street was traveling downhill, I could not see the beginning of the crowd of walkers. As far as my eye could see behind me (which you had to do in a quick glance, otherwise you'd cause a pile up), I could not see the end of the walking crowd. Imagine not being able to see the horizon of the godly before you or behind you. Like a sea of people with no end, everyone was marching in silence to the sound of humility and sorrow, but to God it was a loud cry of love. I never knew that so many were on our side, joined with us in purpose of one accord, and that was an extraordinary feeling. Our prayers were directed on behalf of this nation as we gave way to a broken and contrite spirit for all the evil the nation had laid its hands upon. Such a silent prayer would rock your world, stir you to the core. That experience alone is something I will never forget, but God had a greater deposit for me to receive.

As the repentance walkers arrived on site for the main occasion, word caught on that 70,000 people filled the Titan Stadium in Nashville. The day was dressed with hymns, praise and worship, silent prayer, group prayers, preaching, teaching, repenting, forgiving, and the list goes on. Each part of the day, a different section of national concern or spiritual burden was addressed and prayed over. Abortion and racism were two of the many components of the day. But something different was mentioned that I had never heard of before. In fact, a young male speaker on behalf of a group of youthful prayer warriors began telling a story to introduce the next theme of the day, but they kept the object of the story undisclosed until they had described their real life event.

The story played out that an infant, unwanted by its own parents, was brought to a young group of men and women who were joined together through their own prayer ministry.

Although the group sought after a home for the child, no possible home situation was found, not even temporary placement. The young group of men and women looked no older than their early twenties on the stage, and I assumed none to have been married. One of the young men told how they, in perfect knowledge of the situation and in faith, took this child in and cared for it because there were no other caretakers to be entrusted with the baby. The young twenty-something's took shifts looking after the infant. I imagine some were in college and working while others had full-time jobs, but they juggled their schedules to feed, nurture, and love the child, not knowing ultimately what the Lord would lead them to. It was only a short time later, as the story continued, that a young couple from outside this group who heard of their foster-like situation had hearts prepared to take this child in and become the parents. It was a divine series of events. If the small group of prayer warriors hadn't followed the call and taken hold of faith to keep the infant, these new parents would never have had the baby as their own, and the child would have missed this God-appointed home.

My heart began to rise and fall with the lyrics of the story. I was lifted up in joy, and yet somehow encumbered by an invisible weight I could not pin-point. It wasn't until the next speaker arose and mentioned "the Spirit of Adoption" that I began to understand the subject line of the story and my own swelling sentiment. Immediately, my spirit rang out and my heart finished breaking in correlation with the emotion in the story. I was won over by an invisible force. I remember hitting my knees on that tarp-covered turf and crying out for the children who were left without the miracle ending this child received. I felt deep, slow waves of God's Spirit move into mine. He was changing something in me.

It was no accident that I had heard this story, nor that I made the trek to TheCall in Nashville that year. Everything tied together for me. God was calling my heart to the Spirit of Adoption. A new unfound fervor to see the helpless have a chance in life was awakening inside me. I wanted to see lives rescued, and though my mind tried to, I could not bear to dream up all the children that are continually left by the wayside. Although each focus of TheCall was powerful, something inside of me rang true with this: I needed to get abandoned babes into the hands of mothers and fathers--families that desired a child who needed love. It has been the underlying current inside me since that day. This burning passion has been a constant reminder to me that something must be done on behalf of the unmentioned countless number of children in our nation who are found unwanted. The life-giving force of the Spirit of Adoption is meant to be transmitted to every person, child and adult. It wasn't enough that I heard one inspirational story. I felt compelled to release this vision and heart-dream to others.

CHAPTER

1

The Spirit of Adoption

Cheryti had dreams of Cecilia before she had seen her in pictures or in person. In them, Cheryti saw a young girl set between the eras of childhood and young adulthood. God had given Cheryti faint portraits, like small glances, of her next child in beautiful night encounters, and she hung on to those silhouetted visions with care. When looking through potential children's profiles, she had those images with her, quietly tucked in her heart and mind. One unforgettable feature of the girl in her dreams was a full head of curly hair. When Cheryti and Shawn were looking at Cecilia's profile a lot of things looked wonderful, but one thing kept bothering Cheryti. Cecilia had straight hair. Cheryti had doubts even though they seemed to be moving in Cecilia's direction. At times, she asked her husband if they were doing the right thing. She wondered if this was the right child, but as though God were leading them, they pressed forward anyways.

It took a year and a half from the time Cheryti decided she wanted to adopt her fifth child to the time adoption was finalized and the child was completely hers. As soon as she resolved in her heart and with her husband, Shawn, to have one more, she began her pursuit. Their research began online as they looked through endless profiles of children from the foster care system weekly and daily.

Shawn and Cheryti had already experienced the process when they had previously adopted four children of the same family. The sibling group was split up one from another at one point while in the foster care system. When the couple adopted them, they not only gave their children the wonderful security of a forever family, they also united the siblings in one loving home. It is a gift that not all foster sibling groups are afforded, but it is a powerful blessing to those who receive it. This time however, Cheryti was looking to adopt just one child, and it was going to be different from her past experiences. She and Shawn were looking for a teenager. Educated in foster care and adoption, she knew that the age group of foster children who are least likely to be adopted are adolescents. They are usually considered an undesirable choice and often become the forgotten faces in a land of piled government files. Cheryti, however, was determined to find the one that God had for her.

Taking into account everything that she desired for her fifth adoption, Cheryti began classes and new licensing with the adoption agency of her and her husband's choice. Trainings, paperwork, and a home study were required before she could consider making any legal steps. In the meantime, the searching process lasted a complete year. Over the course of the first nine months, she and her husband looked at countless children's profiles and had considered ninety. A more refined search led them to submit paperwork for just nine children, but after reconsideration and diligent seeking after the Lord's guidance, they didn't have clear certainty about any of those children. So she turned down those opportunities before beginning any course of relationship with them. Finally, at the very end of those nine months, like a woman who carried a child in the womb and then at delivery saw the child's face for the first time, Cheryti saw the profile of a young seventh grade girl named Cecilia. This time after submitting her work, Cheryti got a phone call back from the adoption agency asking if she was still considering adopting Cecilia, and she said yes.

Though the couple couldn't explain the discrepancy of details in the Cheryti's dream with the child they were considering, a presentation meeting was scheduled none-the-less with a few foster care workers and Cecilia's foster mother. Shawn and Cheryti wanted to find out more about the seventh grade girl, and this was perfect place for their inquiries. When the foster mom met the pair, she sat across the table staring curiously at Cheryti. The foster mom finally spoke up explaining that her foster daughter made it habit to straighten her hair with an iron but was amazed that Cheryti's locks of tight curls seemed identical to the very curls of Cecilia's natural hair. For just a moment, Cheryti closed her eyes and drew a smile across her face. Her heart immersed in a wave of satisfaction at the thought of her God dream becoming reality. The fragment of doubt born from the straight hair Cheryti had seen in Cecilia's online profile no longer had any hold on the mind or emotions of these hopeful parents.

Cheryti began visiting Cecilia at her foster home in May, and less than a month later, she was able to have Cecilia over in her own home for a few days at a time. Things seemed to be going well. Cheryti's family was enjoying Cecilia, and Cecilia was enjoying them. With the signs of great expectation, they decided to take the giant next step that would profoundly change the nature of all relationships involved. Cecilia took all she owned and moved in with Cheryti's family in an interim stage called 'adoptive placement'. She was now fully placed in Cheryti's home, but the adoption would not be finalized for another six months as regulations required. It was a fascinating family transformation and a big move for everyone. Cecilia, however, did not have high hopes.

Cecilia was a kindergartner when she was first placed in foster care. Similar to the children Cheryti and Shawn already adopted, she came from a sibling group of four in the foster care system who had eventually been split up to different foster homes. They had reunited under one roof later and then were split up again. By the time Cheryti came along, her three brothers had been adopted together in one family, and Cecilia was still out on her own. She was often moved from one home to another, and she experienced a number of disruptive foster placements and failed adoptive opportunities. Cecilia had received the hope of a family who would finally take her in and love her on more than one occasion only to find out they didn't mean it in the first place when they sent her back into the system. She had been tossed like a rag doll through the hands of so many that she had little left to believe she was worth anything.

Her cynicism only increased through the traumas of the other foster care children around her. In her latest foster home placement where she was living when Cheryti pursued her, two girls of the six total children had just been placed in adoptive homes and both were rejected. Cecilia watched them return back to their foster home without any semblance of a permanent family. When Cecilia left for Cheryti's house under the legal arrangement adoptive placement, the children didn't even bother saying goodbye to her. They simply told her that they would see her later. Their doubt allowed no potential for a happy ending, and Cecilia shared their conviction.

Cheryti was already a licensed professional counselor who typically worked with non-traditional families like single parents, step parent families, and grandparents raising grandchildren. She focused most of her work on foster and adoptive families. Cheryti's expertise came from her direct practice with the situations she counseled. In addition to adopting, she and Shawn had fostered a dozen teenage girls. Her professional work coupled with her experience as a foster parent to many and an adoptive parent to four produced a filling confidence that she could successfully parent her first teenager. Although they knew the work would be difficult, they believed Cecilia's homecoming would unquestionably and unfailingly lead to a joyful ending.

Cheryti's heart had fallen to adoption years earlier when she was just a child. She was the daughter of two American missionaries in East Africa. Hundreds of African children filling the streets were a constant vision before her. Some were orphans to the AIDS epidemic, some were sold into the human traffic sex slave trade, and some were merely in deep poverty whose parents were essentially absent because they were always gone working, desperately trying to care for their family. Young fatherless boys in gangs of 20 or 30 would raid the streets and ruthlessly rob whatever they could take from people and out of vehicles. The most common picture of this sad injustice and childhood destitution was children taking care of children. She saw eight year olds grasping the hand of their four year old siblings, carrying an infant strapped to their back trekking through the streets alone, and yet beside every other child doing the same thing. The images of homeless children carried with her through adulthood. She knew she needed to answer the call of taking in and loving children that others had left and rejected. For Cheryti, there were far too many children crying out on the inside like those African babes in the streets.

When Cheryti finally received Cecilia into her home as an adoptive parent, the sixth month transition of tough times and trying patience began. Fortunately for Cecilia, Cheryti was well prepared. Cheryti had seen so many cases time and time again of prospective parents giving up on children well into the adoptive placement phase. These breaks in relationship only break the children's hearts further. Shawn and Cheryti made a decision to commit to Cecilia prior to her placement; they didn't see the six month wait as a mere trial period. Cheryti stands her ground when she says that every adoptive parent must make up their mind to be committed to the child *before* they enter your home. Even threatening words of being put out of the family are detrimental to the child's trust. Not deciding to commit is often deciding to put another wound on their soul. Cheryti was not one to offer those type thoughts any opportunity; she determined to love Cecilia without fail.

Unbeknownst to all involved, Cheryti lived in the same area Cecilia had grown up. The young foster girl had come full circle as she returned to her hometown, the place she last saw when the CPS workers took her away. Instead of walking into a new life with new surroundings, she was entering familiar places that brought memories of anguish and fear back to life. Because of that, a lot of anger resurfaced towards her biological family, but for her, the biological family was nowhere to be found. So the anger she felt was redirected to her new family. In addition, when she arrived to see the family in Cheryti's home, she saw four siblings who had been adopted together. She had started as one of four siblings, but now that her brothers had already been adopted, realization manifest that she would never live in the same family with them again. That sorrow of dying hope alone brought emotional distress. What arose in her was a conflict of loyalty. She still remembered her original family, and her heart naturally wanted to remain in the place she came from, even in the midst of a possible new life. The jumble of emotion seemed to jumble Cecilia. All of these emotions were a heavy weight and a complex puzzle to manage in the mind of one 13 year old girl.

Cecilia hadn't been in a real family in so many years that she didn't know what to expect or how to act. The only family life she experienced was highly dysfunctional and then extinguished at the tender age of six. A part from not knowing how a healthy family operated, she did not even know what her role was supposed to be. In her family of origin she was the second of four. However, she was the youngest in her most recent foster home, but in Cheryti's family, she made the hard switch to being the oldest. Memories of previous adoptive placements made her distrust the current family, and in her mind there was only a certain line to cross before these parents would send her back too. So she tested the family with defiance and unrestrained outbursts of emotion.

Their new adoptive child came in with the mannerisms of a last born, expecting others to do for her what she claimed she couldn't do for herself. Statements like, 'I can't do my own laundry!' was a sign that she didn't want to try. 'I don't want to sweep the floor!' was an indicator that she was rebelling. Cecilia had fits of screaming and swearing in her new guardians faces, but these tactics only built up Cheryti and Shawn's resolve to be a unified partnership of consistency and love. Cecilia yelled at them saying she hated them and shouted out to Cheryti that she was not her mother. Although Cecilia was able in the beginning to keep her tantrums of emotion at bay half the time, the fits generally went on 3 and 4 days a week.

Slowly light emerged with hints of a new relationship budding. There were indications of Cecilia opening up to the idea of a real set of parents she could trust. When Cecilia arrived at her new home she had a Facebook page where she quickly deleted her previous last name. Her new name simply read "Cecilia". Although, she no longer identified herself with her past, she wasn't quite ready to commit to anything new. She was still caught between the old and the new in a space of peculiar uncertainty. Sometime later, her adoptive parents let her pick a new middle name at her request. Since her new last name would soon come on a fresh birth certificate and social security card, the change to her middle name would be simple. Her Facebook name read "Cecilia Nicole". Her new public announcement told her friends that she seemed to feel like a new person, but she wasn't sure where that new person was landing or who she would be. A few months later during some hard times at home, Cheryti unexpectedly found that Cecilia had changed her Facebook name again. This time she made Cheryti and Shawn's last name her own, and she also linked the two as her parents. Her identity as a member of the family was blossoming.

As time went by, Cecilia began making pieces of artwork for Cheryti and her new dad. She displayed her creativity in the form of love, as though she were reaching out to say she wanted them to know her more. In September after school began, Cecilia was given an art class project painting a portrait of the person of her choice. Without telling anyone, Cecilia chose her new adoptive mom as the subject of her work. When Cheryti had seen the painting, she was touched that her daughter, in her own desire and decided intention and out of all the people she could have chosen, wanted to paint her. Realizing Cecilia was beginning to bond with her, Cheryti felt her own heart draw in closer to her daughter's at the joy of such sweet beginnings. These initial glimmers of hope looked like the promise of a warm family union.

In December of 2010, after floating in the foster care system for some eight years, Cecilia was made the sure and genuine daughter of Shawn and Cheryti. The adoption was legalized, and she became the permanent member of a healthy family. The transition into an atmosphere of continual relationships and love did something tremendous to Cecilia's heart. She poured out her feelings on paper in a poem not long after the finalization. Her words graced the page and reflected the beautiful truth of her own heart turning to her parents, and consequently, she began to sense her identity in a new light. She watched her adoptive parents prove her value as they extended their lives and love to her, and she began to understand their commitment to her meant she was worth so much more than she could imagine. For the first time in a long time, she assigned true value to herself.

Since then, Cecilia has grown in relationship and love with her family. Over the past year, Cheryti has watched her new daughter move from insecurity to confidence that has allowed her to begin new friendships and try out novel activities. The second summer in her family's home she finally agreed to go to summer camp, a huge step forward from last year's fear of being left behind and not seeing her new family again. And at camp, even more apprehensions were overcome. She displayed her courage as she stepped out to ride the zip line, something that was far from possible a year ago. Cecilia's confidence is emerging as her family, the foundation under her heart, steadily proves through time that they are not going anywhere. The girl who was once insecure in many ways and in so many aspects of her life isn't hanging around as much because the new girl is blooming. As to her siblings, Cheryti said this, "My daughter who is a year younger [than Cecilia], missed her every day she was gone to church camp and couldn't wait for her to return home. She counted down the days." Their family continues to blend into one, while the lines of past histories slowly fade. The family that exists now has greater power in each of their lives than the wounded memories of the children's past. Though it requires constant effort, like with any child, the rewards are priceless. Cheryti says true to the ties of love, she and Shawn did not just adopt Cecilia. Cecilia adopted them.

The story of adoption starts with a passion born in the heart of the parents. Shawn and Cheryti didn't begin their journey when they decided to adopt children. Their journey began when their heart picked up the mantle of selfless love.

That passion, that mantle of love is the Spirit of Adoption. The Amplified bible says in Ephesians 1:5 "For He foreordained us, destined us, planned in love for us to be adopted, revealed as His own children through Jesus Christ, in accordance with the purpose of His will [because it pleased Him and was His kind intent]." I love the part that says He "planned in love for us to be adopted". With the same heart God had adopted Cheryti and Shawn in the spirit, Cheryti and Shawn planned for adoption as they scrolled through endless profile pictures. They planned to become licensed foster parents. Their selfless love drove them to take classes and complete all the tedious paper work. God had prepared their hearts with love, and in obedience, they got ready by preparing their home for Cecilia, an unknown child to their eyes but known to the hope of their souls. The couple planned in love to adopt God's child for them.

The New Living Translation says it this way, "God decided in advance to adopt us into his own family by bringing us to himself through Jesus Christ. This is what he wanted to do, and it gave him great pleasure" (NIV). God brought us to himself through adoption, and parents all around the world do the same thing by bringing children to themselves. Helpless as children may be, it will always be our duty to take the initiative in bringing them to us. They will never call us first. They won't write us letters from the streets of New York or Chicago or Dallas. They won't email you from their war torn families to tell you how desperate they are for yours. The bible says, "We love because he first loved us" (1 John 4:19, NIV). The child crying out for love will never know love unless you first love him. The way God's love opened up to you while you were running from Him and yet crying out for help is the way we are called to love these children. The Spirit of

Adoption must so ravish your heart that you are willing to love them at all costs. What the world says is unlovable, God says is worthy to 'decide in advance to adopt'. He brought us into his family. Cheryti and Shawn brought Cecilia into theirs. What will your heart be prepared to do?

Bearing the Spirit of Adoption goes further than wanting a child in your home for your fulfillment; it is loving them for theirs. Hundreds of thousands of little hearts are left wanting in our nation every day. There are millions across the earth. The further we go into the Father's heart, the more we absorb His heart for them in us. If we are to be like Him, then we will no less carry the Spirit of Adoption in us than we carry Christ in us. His heart desire is not that we would only enjoy the blessings of his gift but that we would extend that gift to others. All works of selfless love are God's command to us, but adoption is the ultimate expression of the Father's love. It says *everything* that is mine is yours. You are worth *all* my time, *all* my energy, *all* my money, and *all* my love. The Spirit of Adoption lacks nothing. It is a fulfilling endeavor. The work of adoption releases an inexpressible joy in parents the way it pleased Him to adopt us. I can almost imagine the twinkle in His eye when it says our adoption into His family gave Him great pleasure.

There are nearly 74 million American children living in the United States today, and according to the Child Trend's Data Bank and the National Survey of Adoptive Parents, approximately 2 percent or 1.8 million are adopted whether international, domestic, or from foster care. Cecilia's story is an amazing one, but it is not an isolated case. She represents a mass of children who didn't have a family or the promise of unconditional love but never-the-less was found by one. While a child is born in the U.S. every 7 seconds (U.S. Census Bureau), about 5,000 U.S. adoptions are taking place every day. Those adoptions are like new births to the parents and a new start in life to the child. Families all across our nation with open arms and compassionate hearts, like Cheryti and Shawn, are finding children they desire to bring into their homes. They are determining to love them as if they were always their own sons and daughters.

CHAPTER

Destiny in the Heart of Every Child

Pastor Aaron is a longtime, close friend of my husband's. They met while they both lived and worked for a large church in Louisiana. Aaron is the kind of person who delivers spiritual zeal and intensity everywhere he goes. He is a bouncing source of God energy that rarely quits. My husband, on the other hand, is the more settled wisdom and knowledge deliverer. His natural outward stance is more of quiet confidence and composure. People have always come to him for advice, seeking in him a safe place for help and a source of God insight. The two of them share a kind of brotherly heart bond that is so rarely revealed and appreciated even in relationships where it does exist in society today. I have seen the two of them together at a distance, plunged into the depths of their own world of personal conversation. In those instances, the honor and love they have for one another seems to radiate in the atmosphere around them. One defining characteristic they undoubtedly share is how serious they take their walk with God and their earnest desire to know and love Him more.

Aaron and his wife Amanda love children, and they have fun with their own beyond anything I have seen in a set of parents yet. When I first met them, they had three, and less than three years later, their desire grew their family to five. Pastor Aaron is, in measure with his natural personality, the playful outgoing dad that is just as excited about the new things his kids are seeing as his kids are. As I have watched him interact with his children, he seems to deposit constant nuggets of curiosity and a wealth of passionate enthusiasm into their souls. In effect, his children love to learn, and they are some of the brightest most creative beings my husband and I have come across. Amanda is full of nurturing love and endowed with a quiet but powerful fervor for her children. As her kids played in the living room nearby, Amanda and I spoke in the kitchen one evening when they invited me and my husband over for dinner. She began to reveal to me in a small way the perception of children that she and her husband have that I had never dreamed. While we were talking about one of her children and his tendency toward strength and agilities at such a young age, I highly encouraged her to place him in gymnastics. I expected her to share in my robust support for such a talented youngster, thinking she like any other parent would drool at the dream of a successful and talented child who had the potential to rise above the rest. But her response was more reserved. Without any sense of eager movement, she said that she would consider involving him in the activity, as though she must do some deciphering first. It boggled my mind that a mother would not jump at such an opportunity, but I respected it greatly non-the-less. Later, I connected the dots as my husband told me more about the way Pastor Aaron and Amanda raised their kids. This precious couple contends for God's vision of what their children's lives are destined for, and in that manner, they raise their kids accordingly.

In the general population, the once athletic parent makes their children try every sport until they find the one that makes them an unconquerable athlete. In other instances, musicians made into parents make their child play every instrument and sing in every range until they are musically inclined. Instead of forcing their children to become what ideal they have for them, Pastor Aaron and Amanda seek God for clues of the gifts, talents, and purposes of each individual child. They watch their children's' reactions and pay attention to their developing personalities. In essence, they are seeking God first for an answer on how to parent every child, and they treat each one as a separate and unique gift from God, not as if they are all same. This mind blowing approach changed the way I see children. No longer do I want to see children put in a box expecting the same outcomes for the same treatment. I understand they are supposed to be handled differently and with great care because each one is a distinct gift from God.

Every child has a call on his or her life. Every human being was meant to praise the one true God. Our God is in pure delight when the eyes of a new child open for the first time. He seeks after a child's heart so that child might know Him all the days of his life. What destiny is upon an infant? Or a five year old? Or a twelve year old? Imagine aiding the Father to train up a child in the way he should go so that he would not depart from it. If we look into the face of one boy, could we see he is meant to be a musician to lift harmonies to the Lord's ears and help crowds of worshipers draw close to the Lord? Perhaps the King of the universe has plans for one little girl to open an orphanage in a third world country or train new female believers in an underground church. The Lord might be planning for one life to become the next president or another to merely show love by giving one cup of water at a time. Who are we to know the Lord's thoughts for His creation?

Each child has a life plan set by the Almighty, and God is not going to leave them in the dust. We shouldn't either. Instead, we should see a life or a soul the way God does. The same soul you had when you were one year old and even in the womb of your mother is the very soul that you have today as an adult. It is what identifies you as you. The Lord creates souls and makes plans for them. When he looks at a child, he calls that person by name, not by what stage of development that soul is in. For instance, while we look at an infant and make baby talk, God is calling that child's purpose. When we see a five year old in kindergarten, God is fashioning that child by the experiences, love or lack of love, and circumstances that child endures. We see a 10 year old; God sees a soul. We see teenager; God sees an individual. We see mom and dad; God sees souls. We see an elderly person; God sees a beautiful soul.

When little David son of Jesse was playing with the flocks learning how to shepherd, God saw 'King'. He probably thought 'soul after my own heart'. That is why God could anoint David King over Israel some twenty years before he ever stepped into that position. Our Lord had a very specific plan for this little one who probably rolled around wrestling on the ground with his big brothers. He had a destiny prepared for the one who at first might not have cared to be alone at night watching dad's flocks. God never put this soul in a box seeing just a baby. He saw David for David – when he was an infant, a toddler, an adolescent, and a young man. God saw the soul that was living in the body formed by dust. God saw his heaven-ordained destiny and every talent of his that hid just beneath the surface. He saw David as the potential lover of Himself and as the forever object of His affections.

God sees us as souls because he sees us from our very beginning, the moment he began making us. In Psalm 139, God says so many intimate things. We might blush if we heard them all at once from His very voice. This chapter intricately describes how much care and precision goes into the beginnings of one human life. The words tell us that His eyes saw what we looked like when we were unformed substance (Psalm 139:16). He actually used His own hands to put us together in the womb piece by piece (Psalm 139:13). Our God then fixed His eyes upon us when we had nothing to hide ourselves with – clothes, lies, masks, or otherwise. The word says our frame was not hidden from Him (Psalm 139:15, NIV). If you see the frame of a person, you are probably looking at them bare. Naked. It is a literal phrase that carries immense weight in a figurative sense.

The psalmist is showing us that no matter what we may attempt to conceal from God about ourselves, it is and was always known by Him. Up until this point, the psalmist only describes how well the Lord knows us, but now we find out what he thinks of us. We may not give much thought to the fact that people know us, but how they value you and me holds great weight to us. Knowing how valuable you are to the God that came down and thought about what you might be and look like and sound like is an immense measuring stick to our self confidence and purpose. Some people might whisk that concept away as untrue and go on with life. Others understand the real power behind the Lord's opinion, yet they don't face the answer for fear of the cost of their own possible rejection. Many people look to the left and right, to their bosses, friends, relatives, and pictures of men and women in media for their evaluation of self worth. But the totality of your importance cannot be anymore steadfast than the words of the one who gave you life. This is the bottom line of your existence and reality. No matter what anyone else has said or will say or how others take you in or reject you, you are what He says you are.

Although Christian language paints a pretty picture of who we should assume we are in the Lord, the courageous individual calls upon the Lord in spite of any fear to get his longing answered in an intimate setting. When God finally speaks to your heart, it may sound like this: Though riches make so many happy, I value you above fine gold (Isaiah 13:12). I think you are worthy of royalty, and so I have crowned you with glory and honor, putting all earthly things under your guardianship (Psalm 8:5). I didn't buy you at the lowest price, but I bought you at the highest price to put you under my own tender care (1 Corinthians 6:20). Things you have little value for, I watch day and night. Not one sparrow dies without my knowing, yet you are worth far more than an abundance of them (Luke 12:7). God wants to tell you that you are worth more than all that is around you and that he cares for you over every other thing he has ever created on the earth. Satisfaction might cast over your heart and relief spill in as your desperate yearning is fulfilled. Even when you stand before him naked, bare with all faults visible, he is in love with you. If you were simply to undress your life's pretensions, your many masks of show, your hats of all the roles you play, and laid your life's clothes down, then God would look at you and say 'I love you.' The psalmist knew this exactly! "How precious to me are your thoughts, God! How vast is the sum of them! Were I to count them, they would outnumber the grains of sand" (Psalm 139:17-18, NIV).

He thinks about you. His mind goes back to you again and again, but sand? Sand . . .? Can you even begin to count sand? No, the task is daunting! There is too much of it on just *one* beach alone! How could you possibly understand how much sand is placed on the earth? Why would you even try? I will tell you why. To show you how many times God thinks of you in one day. Try one year. This is an obsessive God. He is in love with you, and he thinks you are worthy of passionate pursuit. He says that you are worth every thought that crosses his mind. Otherwise, he wouldn't waste His time. He is the beginning and the end, and let me tell you, if he *is* the beginning and the end, he *sees* the beginning and the end, and that of you. When we receive this acceptance, then we can really receive all other scriptures that are so common to the ordinary Christian today. Let them sink a little deeper. Let them penetrate the walls of your heart. He knows the number of hairs on your head (Matt 10:30) . . . Does your mother or father know the number of hairs on your head? How about your spouse or best friend? But when you fell in love with that special someone at one time in your life, I bet you knew how many baseball caps he had or what kind of candy was her favorite. You might have known how they liked their coffee or what their mind usually wandered to when conversation fell quiet. Maybe you even finished their sentences.

Understand the difference in level. God numbers the hairs on your head . . . He knows when you get up and when you lie down. When you are far off, perhaps thinking on your own, not talking to anyone else, he knows exactly what it is that is dancing around in your heart or running on your mind (Psalm 139:2). This is the sum of His love for you, apart from what He has done, "You have searched me, LORD, and you know me." (Psalm 139:1, NIV). Who do you know that searched after you? Has anyone sought after you to get inside your mind or to the bottom of your heart? I am going to tell you right now that a lot of your friends like to hang out with you. Some of your co-workers enjoy your company at lunch. Your family desires your energy and spirit. But very few, if any, aim to search you like this. Can you feel the depth of this love? This isn't superficial. Many people live in a superficial love. This is radical love. This is just love because he loves us. We don't even have to go to lunch with Him to get it.

A unique trait God gives humans is the capability to perceive other people in this indistinguishable manner of love. There is a light of eternity that bestows vision in one person to see the amazing value in another. It is like looking through the lenses of God to see what He sees. It usually renders a heart attraction in the life of the first person to the other, but it also instills an immense desire to see growth, success, and achievement in them as well. This selfless overwhelming love that I am describing is most often found in the heart of every parent to their child. Sometimes, however, parents are not able to or choose not to take the responsibility, and a kind hearted individual becomes the surrogate father or mother blessed with a heart bent toward the child.

Such is one story that plays out in February of 1895 when a son was born to two German-American parents in Maryland. The young boy's parents worked hard disciplining themselves to 100 hours of labor every week in the aftermath of a national financial panic. Times were rough for most to begin with, but this couple had more to grieve. They had bore eight children in total but lost 6 of them to sickness at early ages. Their surviving son was a truant, who practiced minor delinquent acts and stole money from the meager family business income for fun not realizing the implication of greater poverty. The burden overwhelmed his parents, and they decided he became far too much for them to handle. Perhaps it was with a mixture of reluctance and relief that the parents took their "unruly" 7 year old to a catholic school for boys in Baltimore. There they relinquished their legal parental rights, and the catholic missionaries took full custody of him.

During the twelve years of his stay, his mother, Kate, would come to visit him nearly every weekend. Sadly, she died of tuberculosis when the boy was only 14. Though his father was still alive, Kate's son never had a visitor for the remainder of his time in catholic school. His father never showed his face to his son. The pain that must have cut the boy's heart from rejection of his father did not promise any hope. However one man, the Head of Discipline, Brother Matthias Boutlier, began to form an amiable relationship with the young mischief. He took special notice and poured into the orphan slowly showing him the way of good character and helping him with his schooling. The young man absorbed what his mentor was offering him, and he became someone of more quality spirit. Brother Matthias decided to invest in something additional when he saw some extraordinary talent. As a coach at the school, he taught the boy to play baseball. They worked on hitting, fielding, and pitching for years. The school was well established in sports, and they had multiple baseball teams from each dorm that played on leagues against other schools. Before long, the young boy became a well-built athletic young man who earned the attention of many local eyes. The relationship Brother Matthias poured into him had widened his opportunity for things he never before envisioned. At the age of 19, the young man signed a contract with the minor-league baseball team, the Baltimore Orioles, and went on to play 21 years in Major League baseball. He won seven pennants, four World Series titles, and was elected into the Baseball Hall of Fame. His name is George Herman Ruth, Jr. or known better to most as Babe Ruth.

At a time when the world was raging nation against nation and America stood on the brink of the first World War, Babe Ruth became a beacon of hope as a legendary icon. The Great War began in Europe on July 28, 1914, and just seventeen days prior Babe Ruth made his debut in the professional league on the Boston Red Sox. His entrance onto the national stage seemed to be destined in perfect timing to lift up a nation that would enter into a vicious fight. While Ruth hit 714 home runs over the course of his professional career, his achievements delivered a sign that the impossible was possible. With every home run he hit, he set victory in the hearts of Americans. His heights of astonishment allowed the minds of our citizens to forget the war for few necessary moments and, at other times, rallied the spirit of our nation in the face of uncertainty and long suffering. Where would the strength of America men and their families have been if they didn't have Ruth's paralleling voice of triumph? When the war was too much, what perseverance would have left the American will if not for an illustration of his continual success? Where would George Ruth Jr. have ended up if Brother Matthias hadn't entered his life? What would he have become if no father's heart poured into this estranged orphan?

There's no telling what destruction or silence would have taken hold of the young delinquent, except that success and personal character would have almost certainly been the path he refused. His heart would have surely been squelched of all hope, leaving behind him the same wasteland of hurts he experienced. He certainly would have not earned the discipline and diligence to become a professional athlete. Americans would have tried turning their hearts into an upward feeling, but without a hero to remind the citizens of the roots of their nation's courage, their efforts would have easily failed. The encouragement of pursuing daily life would have slowly drained, but as history would have it, Babe Ruth was granted a chance. Like a driving current, The Colossus of Clout made his way to the World Series in 1918. He pitched a perfect opener, and extended his World Series pitching shutout to more than 29 consecutive innings. It was a record that would not be defeated for the next 43 years. As if his rise in heroism jolted the heart of the nation forward, Americans and the allied forces put a stop to Germany and World War I just weeks later in November. Let me make myself clear. I don't believe Babe Ruth won us a war, but I do believe that he had specific God-ordained purpose on his life of national scale. The wind of his performance lifted baseball fans all around the country in a time of distress, and the hope he deposited was irreplaceable.

The amazing gallantry of Brother Matthias raised up a no-name kid that should have become a homeless drifter, a drunk, or perhaps a criminal into an all-time American icon. Matthias had to have a stirring hope in the lost young boy. He must have seen some possibility of potential inside the orphan, whose parents openly gave up on him. It was gleaming optimism coupled with generous relationship of a fathering spirit that enabled such a largely unimaginable but highly accomplished future for Babe Ruth. The ballplayer says it best in his 1947 autobiography, "It was at St. Mary's that I met and learned to love the greatest man I've ever known. His name was Brother Matthias. He was the father I needed. He taught me to read and write -- and he taught me the difference between right and wrong." What impresses me most about Babe's words is that his admiration for his mentor had nothing to do with baseball. The key that unlocked this young man's life was not sport. It fell entirely upon the father-son relationship that was based on love. To Babe Ruth, Brother Matthias was the greatest man alive.

All souls, including children, are the direct target of God's love – just like the real life story above. Brother Matthias had eyes to see the worth in young George, and pursued his heart in order to see a finer destiny lived through him, not for the sake of achievement or success but for God-appointed fruition. If we catch the love of God in Psalm 139 and understand the intricacy of his workmanship over us, we will be enabled see others in the eyes of this new kind of worth. This love that is poured out over you and me and our limitless value is the same in the child born today. It is the same value scripted to the child born tomorrow. It is the same for every soul that walks the earth. What is unique about children is that they are made to be poured into. They are pliable, teachable, and they learn something new at every corner. Childhood is a crux of life where so many life paths are highlighted and made available while others are dimmed or destroyed. Proverbs 29:15 (NIV 1984) says, "The rod of correction imparts wisdom, but a child left to himself disgraces his mother." Notice this verse is talking about a child, not a man and not an adult. Babe Ruth may have experienced a lot of hardship in his early years, but his new father figure found him while he was still adaptable to life's experiences. It is because so much in a soul and in a life is formed at childhood that we have the greatest opportunity to direct a destiny in young people and lead them to become the greatest of who they are capable of becoming. It is not a good thing to leave a child to himself. No, good is a father and mother imparting wisdom and love into them.

If it were not for the person or people in your life who imparted into you, would life not have been much different? Some of you had the way of hatred and bitterness imparted to you, and some had love and acceptance. Some experienced the impartation of drugs and alcohol, and others had church and godly values. You may have had no parental impartation because your parents were absent, and so you received the impartation that any person, good or bad, would offer you. These things have shaped you. To many, God miraculously and graciously intervened in what was ultimately the devil's impartation. None of us would ever know of or be where God has us today had He not used key influential people in our lives to radically change our course.

When we look into the world at large, however, we see the misguided multitudes who never received the message that God intended for their soul, and so they have not blossomed into the destiny God would set them in. But He made plans for every heart. Can you see the calling on the human soul? See the value upon a child's life, and call it worthy of pouring every ounce of yourself into. They must be taught, loved on, and cared for. They must know this love, otherwise they will not understand their own value. Without the impartation of love, God's intended athletes become gang leaders. His call of government officials become homeless alcoholics. Girls made to be mothers end up as prostitutes in our local brothels. They will throw away the chance at receiving the blessings of God's destiny for themselves because they don't even believe they deserve it. If they are left alone, they will walk away from this gift because they don't think it is theirs. Sadly, most walk away because they never saw it, even while it is placed at their very feet. Much is at stake when we walk away from them.

It is the role of the parents to formulate the understanding of love and instill value in an infant or child. Wouldn't you relish the opportunity to call out the God-talents in children and nurture those gifts? I tell you that just taking a child under your wing inside your house will completely redirect the course of a lost heart and yours too. Just planting seeds of love and truth while inviting freedom in your home creates an environment where God can work. I believe the church can do this in every child's heart, if only she will not leave any child to himself.

CHAPTER

A Parent's Influence

3

Every adult was once at the mercy and will of a guardian. You were once at the mercy of your caregivers. Every adult did not become what he is today without the help and direction of one set of parents, or in more unfortunate circumstances, multiple sets of parents - perhaps many guardians in the aftermath of abandonment or divorce. Where is our direction set? Where is a child's gaze made straight? Where is destiny spoken into a man or woman? "The Lord will make it happen," you say. Yes, I agree. But when will the Lord ever do something on his own without the role of man? Very rarely. He used Joseph after many trying years of abandonment and imprisonment to rise up and feed his own family who became the tribes of God's chosen. He used Moses to take Israel out of Egypt and Joshua to take them out of the desert. He used David to defeat the Philistines, become a king, and strengthen a nation. He used Mary to birth his son, and her husband, Joseph, to be his earthly father. He could have done any one of those things without our assistance, but history reveals that our Father does not work out His affairs that way. He prefers to employ our lives to accomplish His will. God's intent for a child's development begins in the home, and much of their possible future lies in the hands of parents. This wholesome truth is so evident in human life that both Christians and secularists agree.

The relationship between parent and child is unique beyond any other relationship in humanity. It serves that the purpose behind their connection must be more unique beyond any other purpose in human relationships. God's word conveys the special bond when a father speaks to his child saying, "My son, give me your heart, and let your eyes observe my ways" (Prov. 23:26). In a healthy relationship, parents are drawn to their children, and more than most other desires, they desire to see the strong affection returned. This father gets right to the point of conversation, and like a man with deep fervor says "give me your heart". Indeed the radiant love for his child is like no other love about him. Haim Ginott was a Holocaust survivor, an Israeli school teacher, and child psychologist. He wrote many books on children and parent-child relationships, one of which became a best seller. He is quoted saying "The world talks to the mind. Parents speak more intimately — They speak to the heart" (The December List). The nearness between infant and mother and child and father stirs up pictures of deep love, but it was not instituted by heaven for a sweet cooing of the heart alone. God's construction of this parent-child connection was to bring something good into the child that would blossom in later years. As children's hearts fall into the authority around them, they "observe" their ways, or better described in the context of its Hebrew meaning, the children preserve and protect their parent's ways as an internal monument in order that they may ultimately obey what is passed on to them.

The popular theorist and psychoanalyst, Sigmund Freud, had many thoughts on human development, personality, and the childhood experience. Many of his ideas are thoroughly rejected by modern mainstream researchers and students alike. Some find his theories ridiculous, a figment of personal conjurings contorted to fit his own life's experiences. I tend to agree. Yet aspects of his studies have re-emerged in a positive light. Those in the field have picked out bits and pieces of his principles that stand alone as truth. My husband calls it eating the meat and picking out the bones.

In research and theory, Freud recognized that parent-child relations largely make up the character and personality of the child. He said a child is so affected by his first few early years of experiences that his or her personality is firmly formed by the age of five (Schultz 64). In his theory, Freud outlined five stages of human development. Four of his five stages encompass childhood, and three of them concentrate wholly on the effects of parents on children's lives. Freud's theory places the greatest impact of human personality development in the childhood years. These simple principles show his explicit conviction that childhood so intricately forms the adult. While many details of his theories are distorted by sin and worldly knowledge, he rightly related a child's basic psychological formation back to the parent or the parent-child relationship. Freud indirectly says the parent, or another person, is the basic director of a person's psychological maturity in early childhood. The child's future trajectories are not a solitary creation of the individual.

Pat Robertson said in his book The Ten Offenses that parents are "the authors and preservers of their children" (Robertson 118). In other words, just as God is the author of all creation, he has given parents temporary authority over their children until they reach adulthood to co-author their lives. Every decision that a parent makes to positively affect a child's life will positively affect their child's personal design of character. While the child grows, the parent is given charge to preserve that life not just for existence but for quality. Parents should do more than just feed, clothe and shelter their children so that they can survive; they should bring good morals and values into the home. Pat Robertson goes on to say in his book that a father is "capable of drawing wisdom and authority from God and transmitting them to his children" (Robertson 118). Every God-fearing man and woman wants the personality of Jesus infused in their children. The transmission Robertson describes occurs through the parents and not around them. A viable notice here is that whatever is transmitted to the parents can be transmitted through the parents and to their sons and daughters. That means if one mom has a history of a short fuse and a bad temper and her husband has a history of alcoholism and they have since been saved but never truly overcame these obstacles in their life by surrendering them to Jesus, they will eventually leak out and trickle down into their children's lives, even while they try to hide or suppress them. The same is true for positive influences. A set of parents may have spent their free time at homeless shelters together handing out toiletries and serving food, and their children may inadvertently "observe" and receive that same desire to serve without being taught. Unfortunately, what was transmitted to many was not for the child's good, and it produced an adult who lacked much on the inside and out. Early character and personality is shaped, not exclusively by the natural DNA of the child but by the constant leading traits in parents - hence the phrase, "like father, like son" or "like mother, like daughter".

Karen Horney is another human development theorist who concentrated her areas of theory on love and security. She believed these two forces were the primary motivators in people's lives. Jesus' words and actions confirm this thought. In the gospels He says, "If you love me, you will keep commands" (John 14:15, NKJV). God's ultimate tool for obedience was relationship with him, not just a cold list of rules. He knew that when his children fell in love with him, they would without a doubt follow him. It was out of love us that Jesus stayed the course of God and walked humbly to his death. "When Jesus knew that His hour had come that He should depart from this world to the Father, having loved His own who were in the world, He loved them to the end" (John 13:1, NKJV). The relationship between Jesus and his disciples, all of mankind, and the Father was the motivator of love that allowed him to press in and finish the work set before Him. In her research, Horney saw that the social influences of a child were the greatest determiners of the child's personality. Specifically, she held the socializing process between the child and the parents with the highest regard. She spoke of "safety needs" that she said were higher-level needs for a sense of security and freedom that guarded children from fear (Schultz). The safety needs can only be fulfilled or denied by the way parents treat their child. When parents display a lack of warmth or affection to their child, it feeds the fear factor in them and makes them less secure. Living in a home environment with an absent parent or living in a foster home where the guardian changes erratically can lead to unsatisfied safety needs. Then fear or uncertainty about life and relationships can creep in and alter a child's heart.

Karen Horney took her theory deeper as she described something called "neurotic trends". These are outward actions children may take when they didn't receive a measure of warmth or affection at home. These are naturally produced in children as self-protection mechanisms. When children feel unprotected or unsafe, they work to protect themselves. Horney defined three neurotic trends or ways children react in this type of circumstance. They are 'movement toward other people', 'movement against other people', and 'movement away from other people' (Schultz 166). The first neurotic trend when children move toward people may show up in the form of clinginess, relational obsessions, or open sexual interactions. They just want to feel secure, and so they try to find that person in their life to produce that feeling of warmth they didn't get enough of at home. Horney said she had seen this trend in children as young as the toddlers. The most common instance of this trend today is in young teenage girls who enter into romantic relationships because they are searching for a love they never received. This may come as a result of an absent father, literally or figuratively. Fathers not excepting their role as a father, even while living in the home, is still a missing father, and the son or daughter is still searching for love. Both men and women are searching for something to fill, and they seek it in places it does not exist - other human beings.

I have a friend from high school whose biological father was not in the picture, and her long time stepfather seemed cold towards her without reason. He would often act harshly to her resulting in distrust and even dislike in his stepdaughter's heart. His punishments were callous and on one or two occasions cruel, calling for police involvement. As far as our group of friends had seen, he didn't show her love, and she didn't display any in return. Matter of fact, it seemed more like they avoided each other at all costs. As soon as this churched teen graduated from high school, she left home and began a long string of short sexual relationships moving from one guy to the next as she moved from one party to the next and crashed on a different friend's house for as long as they would let her stay or until she moved on. Her lifestyle was nothing like she had been allowed or taught at home, but her need for something more than rules and judgments from the father figure in her life left her in a season where she was constantly and desperately looking for someone else to fill her heart. Thankfully today, she is happily married, expecting a child, and connected to her local church. Sadly, not all girls who take a turn like hers end up with such a bright future.

The second trend, moving against people, is an aggressive stance children take where anger is the only way to deal in their world. Some children who get caught in this think everyone is hostile towards them. So in order to function, they think they must be hostile as well. Other children are merely angry at their parent's or the situation their parents brought them up in. This can be applied to urban inner city life and gangs. Guns and fights are the only way to make life work. They put up combat one against the other in order to survive. Within the normal family unit, there are the extreme cases of harsh violence, rape, and neglect of basic physical needs such as food and correctly fitted clothing. But what may be more common is simple hostility in the household. Sometimes it is the continual disapproval from parent to child. This is not the disapproval of a child's action, words, or decision, but this is the ongoing rejection of the person. Cold neglect, constant rage, and a lack of support eventually nurture an independent and distrustful spirit in the heart of a child.

The last trend, 'a movement away from people', is a loner position. These are called detached personalities. The children are driven away from any relational ties or emotions so that they can be self-sufficient. Children who walk in this difficulty don't want to draw close to people because getting hurt at home caused their heart to stop trusting everyone. Their basic response was to just shut down in a sense. I believe many mid to upper class, white collared Americans fall in this category. On the outside, they appear successful, but on the inside they are rock hard and unable to let anyone see what they really feel or think. They are often unable to comfortably socialize, and so these individuals may live in the midst of a major downtown city with a driven work ethic in an accomplished career living in a one bedroom apt or a grandiose home involved in no one else's life. And no one is involved in theirs. This is the land of superficiality.

Nicholas Cage played a character like this in a movie that came out in 2000 called The Family Man. In the opening scenes, the prestigious, rich, and single Jack Campbell portrayed a man that had all he ever wanted with no care or need in the world. He moved through his work day in his expensive clothes, drove home in his expensive car, and finished the day in his high-end loft from a bachelor's dream. While the first impressions of his life decorated him as a little conceited, it also tried to make you envious, but it didn't take too long to discover that his life was filled with sin, controlled by work, and horrifically sterile of true relationship. He didn't appear to look lonely by facial expression as he went to sleep alone on Christmas Eve, but you got the idea that if you were him, you might trade it all for one good friend. The character was a phenomenon to me because I didn't expect to see Hollywood portray such a worldly successful person so lonely on the top. The reality is that people who have created a sterile environment for themselves come from every social and financial class imaginable. The effects of this trend show up in adults in more mild situations where an adult appears friendly and might even be outgoing, but deep on the inside they are alone because they purposefully put up walls to fend off intimate relationships due to past hurts. Next time you discover someone that seems to operate like this or in any of the other trends, have mercy on them because they are just as hurt and just as in need as anyone else. This is just what their coping mechanism happens to look like. Your godly compassion may be just the seed that plants love in fertile soil.

A parents' relationship with their child has an amazing impact on every young person's life, and the effects as described above can be lifelong. One sociologist suggests that a positive family environment guided by the parents must be established before the child can truly grow into the full potential he has. Abraham Maslow built a commonly used model of needs that start with the most fundamental needs at the bottom and top off with the most intricate. His theory says the first most basic need people must have is food and water. Once that is taken care of, people can concern themselves with the next most basic need in life – feeling safe and secure. Parents enter on scene in the third level, which is the need to belong. We all want to know where we come from, and we want to make sure we are accepted. "According to Maslow, when the basic physiological and safety needs are satisfied, we can direct our attention to higher level needs: to love, to feel loved, and to belong to our family and community . . ." (Craig 401). How we understand our position in life is determined foremost by personal relationships. The intrigue of his pyramid of needs is what follows. Level four is self-esteem, and the fifth and highest level is the greatest personal achievement of any one person, where he or she fully becomes what he or she is capable of becoming. In a biblical view, this is reminiscent of the plan God has for us in our life, our personal calling and destiny. Maslow calls it 'self-actualization'. Self-esteem says, 'I can do it!' Self-actualization says 'I just did!' It is the manifestation or realization of the fullest potential in ability, skill, and production of any particular person. By listing self-esteem and self-actualization last, Maslow expresses that the family, and the parents especially, are such a foundational mark in human's lives that without their positive influence we wouldn't know who we are or if we are good enough (self-esteem) and would have small chance of accomplishing our God-given destinies and dreams (self-actualization). If he didn't believe the role of parents is not important in guiding children's confidences and destinies, his theory does.

In his book No More Cotton Candy my pastor, Jim Hennessy, writes about an amazing experience he has with his father that yielded immediate results. Of course, good parenting is meant to give the child lifetime rewards and this life lesson did that as well, but it also produced success in him that synchronized with real godly confidence.

As a six-year-old boy growing up in Montgomery, Alabama, I had earned a reputation as the worst baseball player at Flowers Elementary. Whenever I approached the plate, I led the Flowers Blue team in strikeouts. I just couldn't understand why God gave some kids the ability to hit and throw and not me.

When our family relocated to Columbus, Georgia, my father took me to meet my new Little League coach. The coach asked my dad if I was a good baseball player. "He's great!" my father said. At that moment I knew my father was either a convincing liar or a man of great faith. "Terrific - what position does he play?" the coach asked. Dad replied, "What position do you need?" *Now, we're both in loads of trouble*, I said to myself. The coach scratched his head, saying, "I could sure use a starting pitcher for today's game." Dad didn't hesitate to offer my services, even though my pitching experience was limited to playing catch with him in the backyard. "You're in luck – Jimmy is a great pitcher," he said.

When I marched to the mound on our first practice, panic set in. *We're both going to be called liars*, I told myself. I'm not sure if it was Dad's faith or my prayers that converged on that mound, but something supernatural happened. I threw a perfect game. And from that day forward, I became an above average baseball player.

My dad believed in me, and his faith and encouragement changed my game.

Children are inclined to believe what they see, hear, and experience for better or worse. As a young boy, "Jimmy" experienced disappointment in his own ability to play a sport that he loved dearly. His worth in the game was determined by his own record – until his dad interjected. When Mr. Hennessy stepped out by faith and in love and when that faith saw real tangible results, the little league player stepped into a new sense self worth. He decided he was significant enough to the game and his team to continue pursuit of the same results. As he said, "From that day forward, I became an above average baseball player." His success in baseball actually manifested through Little League and into high school. But it all started when his father stepped in with hearty commitment to his son.

Pastor Jim's father had faith in his son regardless of his success or failure. That faith was born out of love, and Mr. Hennessy loved his son without condition. Carl Rogers, my most favorite of theorists, highlighted a major make or break point that occurs in the early years of a child. Rogers posited that acceptance, love, and approval from others are without a doubt, the most imperative point of development. He even gave it a unique name, Positive Regard. When a parent regards their child with any of these quality responses the child is satisfied at the heart. When a parent unconditionally gives the child acceptance, love, and approval uninhibited by the child's actions, Rogers calls it Unconditional Positive Regard. Unconditional Positive Regard is established in the parent-child relationship when love "is not contingent on any specific behaviors . . . It is given freely to children for who they are regardless of what they do" (Engler 350). This sounds a lot like the way Jesus taught us to love one another. He said we are to forgive each other "up to seventy times seven" (Matthew 18:22, NKJV). Jesus didn't say we should love each other if this or when this happens. In fact, we are supposed to love our enemies without stipulation, and if we are supposed to love our enemies in this way, how much less should we love our children? Rogers believes that a child who is loved like this is free to develop his personality and life to the fullest. The child learns to love himself through all circumstances. When a parent does not show Postitive Regard consistently and fails to make the child feel loved, he or she tends to get hurt. In such circumstances where the parent only shows favor or love to the child when the child does what he ought, the child is only loved or accepted when he performs according to the parent's standards. At all other times, the child is rejected. At this point the child learns Conditions of Worth. Their thoughts may be, "I am only worthy or valuable when I do xyz." So the child strives endlessly to accomplish the goals or walk on the pins and needles set out by the authority so that they might earn love. This can also be thought of as conditional love. Regardless of any child's circumstance, the point of common conviction is that childhood is the crux stage for development into adulthood, and parents are the main hosts of this stage in life.

In a book Dr. James Dobson wrote many years ago entitled, <u>What Wives Wish their Husbands Knew about Women</u>, he addresses the low self esteem that many married women struggle with in their day to day life and overall identities. The female inquirer asked Dr. Dobson how feelings of inadequacy creep into the lives of women. She goes on to tell that she is not sure where it all began in her own life. Dr. Dobson replies:

You don't remember it because your self-doubt originated during your earliest days of conscious existence. A little child is born with an irrepressible inclination to question his own worth; it is as "natural" as his urge to walk and talk. At first, it is a primitive assessment of his place in the home, and then it extends outward to his early social contacts beyond the front door. The initial impressions of who he is have a profound effect on his developing personality, particularly if the experiences are painful. It is not uncommon for a pre-kindergartener to have concluded already that he is terribly ugly, incredibly dumb, unloved, unneeded, foolish, or strange. (p36-37)

Dr. Dobson explains that even though his book context was focused on married women, the source of this particular topic did not begin in marriage. It begins as a very young child. While the parents are busy doing life, the infant, baby, and eventually toddler is watching every signal, listening to every tone, and waiting for any response to define what he should believe that he is. And with every motion or lack there of from the parent, the child finds out what he is made to be. It is from these years that the drastic direction of his ambitions, his purpose, and his heart are created.

In every environment something will always be a strong guard and something else will always give way to that guard. In a safe and God-loving home, a child has the freedom to be at peace. He can trust what is around him. That is because the walls are stable; they are his strong guard. Mom is not going anywhere, and she is consistently there. Dad is not going anywhere, and he is predictable. Siblings sleep in the same beds every night. His place of rest does not change from week to week or month to month. This is his strong guard, and what gives way is his heart. His heart can be free. He is at ease, and hopefully, by God's favor and grace, always will be.

The child whose environment is unpredictable, irrational, or inconsistent will suffer from it. The child whose surrounding parents or guardians do not stand as a wall stand to give way, and the thing that becomes the strong guard is the child's heart. There is no more play involved. Now it is a fight. Now survival is the mode of operation - not love, not creativity, not engaging relationships. The child's life direction has been redirected. This child is not focused on enjoyment or his future. He is fixated on the here and now. How can he get by for himself since nobody else is looking after him? It is fear that ultimately does the damage. The lie says 'no one else is for you; so you must always be on the lookout for yourself.' A child is reared in the home. He is tattered in the streets. Soft hearts are made in stable homes. Hard hearts are made in unstable environments.

It is a sad state when one is "left to himself" as we saw in Proverbs 29:15 in the previous chapter, but it is a joy and a beautiful thing when a child is brought up to understand him or herself in relationship to the Lord and the world. Both Proverbs 10:1 and 15:20 say that a wise son brings joy to his father. How does that wisdom come? All wisdom comes from God, but that wisdom is most commonly transferred from the parent to the child. Proverbs 1:8 says, "Listen, my son, to your father's instruction and do not forsake your mother's teaching." God so readily shows us his way of doing things. Even the unsaved and the learned in the world, like the others mentioned above, can see the way personality and hearts are shaped. God wants to move through the hearts of the parents to reach the hearts of the children. What a humbling thought that God wants to move through our hearts and souls to transform theirs. He made the world so that His work would reach through us to touch someone else.

What happens to the child untouched by the gentle love of godly parents? Who is the child that is put in an orphanage or is taken away from home because of parent's lawlessness or given up to the streets in poverty? Let's peer into the life of their heart. The next section is a monologue of that child, the voice of a child whose parents did not play that imperative role of love and loyalty in their life.

> I don't know where I come from, and I don't know who I am. My parents have left, at first just in action, and then in heart. Well, I wish that was my story. I was actually left as a toddler in a third level apartment hallway. They said I was a scared little guy and crying. I have never known love of unconditional fervor, and I have never been taken in. It would have been cool if I got a different foster mom, but she just laughed at me and my plans. So then all the other kids did too. It was difficult to live alone and be my own guide. I was not sure I would make it, but somehow I survived. I told myself I could do it – running away I mean, and my friends told me, too. We said we could do anything. It was every man for himself so that we could make it through. I was just looking for a home, a real one, where I could tell people about my plans. Maybe they would even go hit the ball with me for a

while. I always wanted go to a real ballpark so I could see my home team from the stands.

I don't know my real last name, but I have always wanted one and a place to run to when I am weak and tired. Will you give me an identity? A family name I can cling to? Can you tell me who I am? I am lost and have no way. I really don't know where to go, but I was hoping you could point me in the right direction. I heard I was made for love, but since no one showed me, my heart grows cold and distant in my teenage years and harder yet still as a grown adult. Now you have waited too long and the devil has stolen and the world has planted. And all I ever knew was that I was good for nothing and there was no salvation. If there was, someone would have saved me by now. If only you'd have stooped down low to pull me out of the pit, I'd believe in saving. Now I only live to steal.

I have to get my pride from somewhere; so I take from others what I can. I am a cold person and desperate, too. But you will only see desperation if you look closely in my selfish ambitions and self-centered desires. I strive to keep the real me hidden because I really just hurt deep down on the inside. My heart is all broken and cut up. But half the time I don't pay attention to why I feel the way I do. I don't even understand my own emotions. I expect to find nothing and have nothing good in life. It is the life you handed me when you turned and walked away. Or should I say you just never showed up? Good is something that makes me feel better when I can't push the pain out. What I call good, you call sin and then condemn me for it all the same. I don't know Christ or whatever it is he offered. But look! You will see if you open your eyes I have become a generation of men despised, running rampant in your streets, some redefining morale, some living lawlessly, and some wasting away alone. If you do not love me now, you will soon find yourself fighting me later . . . in your neighborhood, in your government, or in your church.

This is your choice. Would you invite me in? Maybe when I was an infant? Will you look the abused teen in the eye? Can you find it in yourself to chance a kid in your house when you say you don't have enough? I see what you have, and if I had that, I would be a king in a dying world. I needed you to help me. At least help the kids who try to call me dad. Here, I can't do this. Will you take their hand?

The Orphan Spirit

The renowned theorist and psychologist, Erik Erickson struggled ruthlessly with his own identity as he grew up in the European states. Erikson's biological father fled the scene before he ever met him, and he grew up confused about his real surname under his step father's care. Although he was Jewish by his mother's bloodline, his Jewish peers rejected him for his Nordic features, his tall stature, and his blond hair. His German friends rejected him because he had a Jewish mother and step father (Schultz 208-209). He felt as though he had no heritage to turn to. The two bloodlines that he knew of only reminded him of the doubt and shame others drove into his soul. He merely wanted some acceptable identity.

Later as an adult, he moved to America; he took the opportunity to leave all behind him in order to connect to an environment and society that would acknowledge and legitimize him. Still finding no true identity to set his heart upon, he took on a surname that redefined him according to himself: Hence, Erik Erikson. In a memoir to her father, the daughter of Erikson wrote that her "father suffered terribly from the sense that his real father had abandoned him and had never cared to know him" (Bloland, 2005, pp. 52, 71: Schultz 209). It was this identity crisis Erikson bore throughout his life that spurred an interest to research the hunger of his assurance behind it. Becoming a well-known scholar for his work in human development, he seemed to be ever-searching for the person he longed to become. On the outside he was given a family and yet had rejected them for the rejection he had suffered. The fatherlessness he felt on the inside was the medium that shaped him as an orphan at heart.

The word 'orphan' is only listed 6 times in the bible, 4 times in the Old Testament and twice in the New Testament, but the word 'fatherless' is listed 39 times, and all of these are in the Old Testament. I believe the word 'fatherless' isn't mentioned in the New Testament for one very large reason: Jesus. We were spiritual orphans blind to the truth, and when our Savior bore the weight of our sins and died for us on a cross, He became our Lord. And God became our father. So now we are no longer children of darkness. We are no longer parentless. We are no longer orphans. The new concept in the New Testament has to do with God as *Father*. We are putting old things behind us. The old is gone and passed away.

The reason why I bring up the term 'orphan' is for one reason: without full understanding of the former, we cannot have full understanding of the present and the future, and without knowing where we came from, we cannot appreciate where we have been delivered to. Secondly, no matter what country we live in or what city we may visit, there are orphans all around. In the spiritual we have been made part of a family, but in the natural both Christians and non-Christians alike are found without loved ones to call on. The Hebrew word for orphan or fatherless is "yâthôm" which at face value is interpreted as fatherless or orphan, but the Hebrew word's root is a little more poignant. The raw definition is 'to be lonely or a bereaved person' (E-Sword). This hits the issue a little harder for me. Its description alludes to a more personal testimony of the orphan. The definition just went from factual to intimate, and we no longer just know what the person is, we get to take a peek into what they experience.

Jack Frost is an international speaker and minister out of South Carolina. He and his wife Trisha operate an amazing ministry that touches the hearts of people all over the world called Shiloh Place Ministries. One of his most popular and life-changing messages is surrounded on the Father's heart and the contrasting orphan spirit. His teaching on the *Father's Love* is transforming hearts around the world again and again, mine included. He is truly a forerunner in the church's present-day awakening to the spirit of adoption. In his teaching *From Slavery to Sonship*, he relates spiritual orphan-hood to a real life orphan spirit that is contracted by the relationships we draw from in the home. When we own an orphan spirit, he reveals, "We are left feeling that we have no safe place, no one to care for our soul, no one we can trust to affirm and admonish us, no place to belong and be protected." All of these defining emotions are relationship based. The orphan's concern is tied more closely to the desire of love and community than it is to stuff. Generally, it is more about a hole in his heart than his stomach or his wallet. The word fatherless in the bible describes just that.

Seeing the structure of the Hebrew word takes into account what value the Jewish culture put on the family and the father. The American word is defined more by the circumstances the child is in – i.e. a child deprived by death of one or both parents; one deprived of some protection or advantage. Our American and all around western culture sees an orphan or fatherless child has having been deprived of some*thing*. The Israelites saw an orphan first as a child who is deprived of some*one*. The American definition sees the situation as having lost objects like money, clothes, and food or objectives like human protection and provision. The Hebrew definition sees a lost relationship. The difference is vast. It is important to note that God and his people knew that a child without a parent needed material things to cover the first mode of operation – survival, and God is in the business of taking care of the orphan, which we will see in chapters to come. However by the word's direct definition, material need was not the Hebrew's primary mention. Trusting in God and his ways meant knowing that material needs were the last things to fret over. Loving people is what is and always has been God's most vital concern.

The orphan in Hebrew culture is pictured as someone who has no one else. This former son or daughter is lonely. They are without their normal means to live and enjoy life. The definition of bereaved is someone who *suffers* the death of a loved one (Webster.com) or is *grieving* over the death of a loved one (Neufeldt, p131). The word yâthôm is not the equivocal translation of a person who does not know where he will live or where his next meal will come from. It does not primarily characterize the orphan as someone who is lost, scared or deprived of the material necessities of life; although, these things are most commonly the feelings and situations orphans experience. This is the description of someone who is destitute in spirit and has a broken heart. The word choice of this culture reflects the attitudes and values of the culture, and as evident in the language, the value of relationship trumped the concern for provision. Specifically, God's people valued the parents and the indispensable relationship children had with them. The father and protector of the family was more than just the bread-winner in the house; he was the joy of the house.

While doing research, I came upon a verse I had never read in a particular context, and it jumped out at me with a new revelation. Proverbs 17:6 in the New International Version reads "Parents are the pride of their children". I thought to myself, 'I must have glazed over this verse for years', but it is so pivotal to understanding fatherhood and thus the orphan. I think I must have seen this verse all these years exactly backwards from its written meaning! The way families 'do business' today has so much to do with edifying the child. My preconceived thoughts stemming from my culture-shaped mindset made my eyes to read that children were the pride of the parents, and actually scripture does back that. I can't forget how I have always heard from the lips of my mom and dad while growing up "I am so proud of you". Yet this verse is saying quite the opposite.

If we could look back and see what our parents have truly accomplished in their lives or have overcome in the name of Christ or what they did to keep their family as one, we might be the more likely candidate to wear the badge of honor with our parents plastered to it, instead of seeing the soccer mom's wear their child's face on a button. I am not saying it is wrong to honor your child, but this verse describes how important it is for each of us to honor our parents. In the majority of subject matter on rearing children and building family, the scriptures do no focus on parents honoring their children. On the contrary, honoring the parent is the first commandment that comes with a promise from God. Deuteronomy 5:16 says ""Honor your father and your mother, as the LORD your God has commanded you, so that you may live long and that it may go well with you in the land the LORD your God is giving you." The one-way trajectory of honor from child to parent, and not the other way around, is more than a principle, it is a commandment.

This same verse in Proverbs reveals more in the New King James Version. It reads, "And the glory of children *is* their father." I can see a child lifted up and hopeful because of his father - who he is and what role he plays in the home and community. His face might beam in full radiance because, if he was to show off anything, he would love to show off his father - perhaps the man's accomplishments but probably his character and heart. That is glory setting on the demeanor of a child or the deposition of a young adult. It is the way this particular family function was originally intentioned to operate. It is a seemingly trifle thought in the mind of a child to hold back gratitude toward the parent on a small momentary grudge. But whether young or old, this scenario and others like it, can lead down a slippery slope where Christians stop fighting for their families and buy in to the lies of the enemy that says there is nothing worth complimenting in the lives of their parents. Our enemy has come to disrupt and destroy obedience to the fourth commandment. The reason is that it comes with a blessing, if we will stand firm and adhere to it. Satan himself will do anything to hinder the blessings of God. He is the one who comes to steal, kill, and destroy.

If the glory of a child is his father, then it seems only reasonable that Satan would only want to take our fathers away so that we lose our glory. He is, after all, the one who steals. If he cannot steal our blessing by pushing a dishonoring attitude on us toward our parents, then he will steal our glory by taking our father outright from us. If the child buy's into Satan's lie, the child will even begin to hate, condemn and curse the father he never knew. Now the devil has by way of deceit, caused the son or daughter, whether child or full grown adult, to forfeit that promise of a blessing. They have lost their glory because they have taken on orphan-hood by an orphan spirit, and they have lost their blessing because they operate in unforgiveness and a bitter heart. However, the one who merely dishonors the parents that are present in their life, regardless of the parents' heart or actions, is not far from owning the orphan soul as well. Satan will work to grow and develop the prideful spirit of judgment and rebellion until the child has fully rejected their parents in mind, action, or both. Rejecting a parent is like denying them the position they were given by God. It is declining to make yourself the child. It is a divorce by mode of thought, and where there is no father or mother, there is an orphan. How do you find out if you have been tainted by the orphan spirit? Looking at the orphan will demonstrate the characteristics of the person. We can lay down whatever remnants of the orphan spirit have clung to us for something far greater.

Orphans are portrayed as wallet snatchers and dirty ragamuffins in old 1950s movies. They are the "street rat" of the day. Usually bundling up with their immediate brothers and sisters or finding other homeless and lost children to cling to. They might even be working for a cruel man who pays them a penny for every bundle of apples they steal. Fast forward to modern day culture, and the orphan looks a little different. Maybe his mom left him and his dad is in jail. Maybe he never met his dad who ran away long before he was born and his mom committed suicide. But suddenly we see the picture of a child without a family and he hangs around other's who have no idea who their fathers are. In fact, they may eventually live together, and to make things work, they might steal . . . quite a bit actually. And they may find themselves selling illegal substances for a cruel man in charge to get some false shred of safety. These children always find themselves running, stealing, fighting, and looking for a way to escape. Yet no matter what they do in striving and scrounging to make ends meet, they are always hungry because their effort never quite satisfies.

Orphans will spin their wheels to make it in this great big world. They are not provided for whether that is in their emotional needs, physically needs, or both. This ill feeling of unsecure livelihood creates almost a panic mode in their heart. As they search for some sort of provision, protection, or emotional regard, they often find there is no one else to lean on. Still the basic mode of survival requires that someone provide for them. The end result is that they provide for themselves. The independent mindset that develops thereafter leaves them in a place of constant striving. It is a place without rest. As a child learns to lean only on himself, it teaches him as an adult to never enter into or trust a healthy interdependent relationship. Orphans may rest physically, but inside they are always on the move because there is no home for them. They trust no one, and so they can never relax. Sleep is never peaceful. Being 'calm and collected' on the outside does not mean peace on the inside, and it does not mean their work is done. This person is always on the run because no one place is actually home. He has never had a home and therefore does not have an example from which he knows how to create one, enjoy one, or accept one, even when it is handed to him. Rarely can this person receive, and if they do, they act as if they are taking it by force.

The orphan is always stealing because he has nothing of his own. That is all he knows to do. We even see grown adults do this. They may struggle indefinitely with receiving gifts in genuine gratitude, but they may find it natural to try to take others' ideas, friends, or rewards. The orphan does this because he never had a father give to him or provide effectively for him where it comforted his heart. The only way this person knows how to live is to get what he has by taking it. In his mind no one will ever give him anything.

The orphan will find himself fighting, and often times he is fighting himself. To get what he needs, he steals. And if he is caught stealing or offending someone in process, he'll be face to face with opposition. This might be a literal kid stealing his neighbor's bike, or it might be a white collared employee stealing his co-workers marketing idea and taking full credit for it. If found out, the orphan will be in a fist fight or an ugly confrontation. The orphan is going to take what he can, and he will probably be found fending off others to get it. But the orphan will stand to fight because he does not know or understand love since he has never received it, and sometimes just because someone is given something, even love, does not mean that it was welcomed at the other end.

The orphan may be elusive in relationship or hard to get know. Everything around him is a perceived eminent danger. He does not have reason to openly trust anyone, and he does not try. He is always escaping what looks like a trap to him. Every situation is skeptical, and not worth two feet forward. The orphan always has one hand on the door knob and only one foot in the doorway. A fast escape route is always a prepared option. The orphan will not take too risky of a chance.

Of course, we know that we cannot satisfy our own hearts. Humans cannot satisfy the spirit. Only God can. Literal orphans and people with orphan spirits may have this in common: they always yearn for more, but they are never filled. No matter what they steal or what conversation they escape, they can never provide the rest and peace of a home, which an earthly father provides by his love on earth and the Heavenly Father provides in our hearts from Heaven. Jack Frost teaches in *From Slavery to Sonship* that the self-image of a satisfied son or daughter is affirmed because of the value they have in their heavenly Father and hopefully through their earthly father, but the heart of an orphan has self-rejection as its main mode of operation. Since no one accepted them, they choose to not accept themselves.

Here is one example in the Old Testament where the writer employs the word orphan to describe the feeling of his current situation. The book of Lamentations is a book of poetry that describes the horrible destruction of Jerusalem and the judgment and exile of the Jewish people on their way to Babylon. The beginning of chapter 5 tells us their exact position.

Remember, O LORD, what has come upon us;
Look, and behold our reproach!

Our inheritance has been turned over to aliens,
And our houses to foreigners.
We have become orphans and waifs,
Our mothers *are* like widows.
We pay for the water we drink,
And our wood comes at a price.
They pursue at our heels;
We labor *and* have no rest.
We have given our hand *to* the Egyptians
And the Assyrians, to be satisfied with bread.

(1-6, NKJ)

You can see these people feel like orphans because they call themselves just that. They are pictured running in verse five. "They pursue at our heels; We labor and have no rest." Here they are running, not just from the enemy, but they are striving to have any peace, yet they are found without any rest. They must escape the real eminent danger everywhere they turn. It is even difficult for them to get food. "We hunt for food at the risk of our lives, for violence rules the countryside" (Lam 5:9, NLT). They are hungry, and these people are so hungry that they have turned to the foreign lands of their enemies to get some physical relief. "We have given our hand to the Egyptians and the Assyrians, to be satisfied with bread." (Lam 5:6, NKJ)

The people are in desperation. They have nothing, and it doesn't look like they will be given anything anytime soon. Verse three says that they "have become like orphans and waifs". The definition for waif is "anything found by chance that is without an owner; a person without home or friends, especially a homeless child; a piece of property found but claimed by nobody." (Neufeldt, p 1500) Imagine being so rejected that while everyone can see you plainly, being found, no one will claim you. Erik Erikson felt this way, and this is how God's people felt. In fact, they didn't feel like God's people at all because they felt like God had left them. They had become fatherless and without an owner. It was as if to them God refuted being their owner any longer. At the end of chapter five, the writer cries out, "Why do You forget us forever, And forsake us for so long a time? . . .Unless you have utterly rejected us"(Lam 5:20,22 NKJ). These words are an earnest plea from Israel for their father to come back.

Jesus experienced this same desperation. Verse twenty of the previous scripture sounds strikingly familiar to the words Jesus spoke the last day of his earthly life before his death on the cross. Jesus found himself before a crowd of Jews who were his own, but who cried out "Crucify him, Crucify him!" Not even a close disciple of his would claim him in those last hours. Peter, although he was an intimate friend of Jesus and had dedicated the last three years of his life to learn from and walk with the Messiah, denied knowing Christ three times before the sun came up that day. John wrote in the first chapter of the gospel he penned, "He was in the world, and the world was made through Him, and the world did not know Him. He came to His own, and His own did not receive Him." (John 1:10, NKV) Jesus was rejected by the very world he created. His own people would not claim him. His close follower of three years would not say that Jesus was his friend and teacher. Jesus was without a home in relationship, in trust, and within his circle of friends. He probably felt the full weight of complete rejection and abandonment.

To all who are orphans in life or in heart, Jesus knows your pain and internal shouts for help. He has experienced the same abject misery of abuse when he was whipped beyond human recognition, the same rejection when in a time of horrific distress his loyal friends said with their own lips they didn't know Him, and the same torturous abandonment when his dad turned his head away from him in his dying moments. These are the same wounds and scars that you have lived with and harbor in your heart. The bible doesn't exaggerate when it says He was truly a man of many sorrows. He came, in part, to live your pain.

As Jesus hung on the cross he cried out, "Eloi, Eloi, lama sabachthani?"—which means, "My God, my God, why have you forsaken me?" (Mark 15:34, NIV 1984) Jesus felt God turn from him in this dark hour, and for that moment Jesus became like the fatherless. He hung on the cross in an orphan-like state. The glory of the one true Father was something Jesus had to relinquish in obedience during those hours as he bore the weight of all man's sin upon the cross. The scripture says that "For He made Him who knew no sin *to be* sin for us, that we might become the righteousness of God in Him." (2 Cor 5:21 NKJ) At the same time the sinless man was carrying our burden, the Son whose Father was God, became fatherless and orphaned, that we may never have to live as orphans again.

Before Christ came, we were enemies of God. Though not consciously, we were orphans - snatching, stealing, and fighting. Unfortunately, those words sound more like the actions of Satan, and that is what brought us to the status of 'God's enemies'. If we stand in this position, then we have not yet surrendered to Him, and He has not become our Father. But while we were yet sinners choosing to reject God, He had compassion on our dirty ragamuffin faces and hardened hearts. He came to die on a cross for us. You see, we were both lost and unwilling to be found before Christ. We were both an enemy and an orphan. Each goes hand in hand with the other. The man who does not accept Christ is the man who has rejected him. In that rejection, he has become God's enemy. Matthew 12:30 says, "He who is not with Me is against Me, and he who does not gather with Me scatters abroad" (NJK). God longs to bring all that are His close to Him. He wants to gather us to himself. Jesus cried out to Jerusalem while he was on earth "Jerusalem, Jerusalem, you who kill the prophets and stone those sent to you, how often I have longed to gather your children together, as a hen gathers her chicks under her wings, and you were not willing" (Luke 13:34, NIV). But God was the only one who could and would cover you. He is the only one who would take you into His house so that you might have a real home with no mind games and no striving.

Rejecting God is accepting your orphan-hood. It is siding with your own loneliness and depression instead of Him. Saying no to Christ is saying yes to your own circumstances and destiny as they are. This is true uncertainty, but Psalm 91:1 says "He who dwells in the shelter of the Most High will rest in the shadow of the Almighty" (NIV). Receiving salvation means rest. It means security in whomever's shelter you choose to live. And of course, God has the best. Receiving this dwelling means security without worry or fear. It would be as if someone plucked you up as a grown adult out of your current situation and set you in a house where none of your problems are yours;

they are your Father's. They are God's. He makes your food. He feeds you. He brings you opportunity. He pays your bills. He provides you with friends and family. Nothing is ultimately your responsibility. It is all His. That is why God calls the saved His children. Any infant can do nothing for himself. A five year old is almost helpless alone. It is the parent who does all things for him. God is and has been calling us to that place. It is a place of total dependency on Him so that we look more like Him, at peace and full of love, instead of like the devil, who works out his own affairs to the hopelessness of his own anguish and frustration.

God never created us for orphan-hood, but we have the option to walk and die in it. Ultimately, that is what hell is: orphan-hood embraced. The orphan soul is the only one who cries indefinitely in his own pain. God made us to rest in Him, to walk beside still waters and lie down in green pastures so that we would not be wanting in any area of need (Psalm 23). If He gives us everything, then we literally need nothing, and there is nothing we could possibly want. He wants to absolve the orphan spirit in us and make us His own forever.

CHAPTER

Fathered

A grassroots Christian worship singer-songwriter has attracted countless souls with his raw style and honest lyrics. I remember when I first heard his music. It was like taking in a breath of fresh air that I never wanted to let go. His spontaneous words and spirit-led melodies leave many a heart undone. He touches the human soul almost effortlessly because he says what we are really thinking and gives the answers we really need to hear. In a song entitled Father of the Fatherless, he sings:

> How many sons have cried for their fathers?
> And how many fathers have cried like a son?
> Now every tear saved through the years in memory's bottle
> becomes the fine wine you serve to the children of God.

Jason Upton is the man behind the words. I think the unsaid, heart-wrenching longing between his lines is that we all just want a father, a real, loving, believe-in-you-till-you-make-it father. This talented, God-inspired musician was adopted by a set of, as he says, "sweet" Christian parents before he was old enough to talk. His intimate knowledge of the Spirit of Adoption with heaven and his earnest desire to see all of us come to that understanding is a ministry every song of his seems to run with.

Why would a child cry out for his father, except that he desires the protection of the tall, unhindered fortress of a giant super hero that he calls dad? When you are six, no one person is impenetrable like your father. No one can fix everything or know everything like he does. No one can rescue from the terrors of nightmares or the sting of a bee. No one else owns your trust like him. Over time childhood changes, and the perspective we once had of our father alters into something much different. We watched him falter. We saw him fail a time or two. We caught wind of his weak spot, and we calculated his humanity to be as natural as our own. No more super hero dad, except that he might still be the honored super hero of your heart. You found yourself coming to respect the 60 or 80 hour work weeks he took to feed the family, the decisions he made for your benefit, and the sacrifices he wore with dignity. Perhaps his faithfulness or his character is what you admire. But why would this man – your father, as Jason Upton put it, cry out like a son? When their earthly fathers are no more, when they pass from this life, when their deeds didn't measure up to expectations, or they have failed us completely, the grown man still has a place in his heart that only a father can fill.

This cry inside the human heart sung in the lyrics above yearn simply for love, and only one person in our entire life can instill such a magnificent satisfaction. The bible simply puts it, "What a man desires is unfailing love" (Proverbs 19:22, NIV, 1984). Try as we may to fill our own hearts, neither romantic relationships, nor siblings, nor friends, nor euphoric experience can do in our hearts what a father was made to do – not even a mother. Our hearts cry out for protection and approval, comfort and affirmation, guidance and love. There are far too many traps in this life that take us away from what our heart tells us we long for. And often times we go out in search of something to plug up this endless cry in our heart. After we have tasted sin's falsely advertised potions and remedies, what is always offered to us is the seemingly long walk to the Father's house, which is ultimately His heart, that place of unfailing love.

I can see the prodigal son in Jesus' parable striding that long stretch home wincing from the reeling thoughts in his mind of the words his father might say after he had done everything possible to embarrass himself and his father. The son drug his feet and loosely scuffed the dust every couple of steps out of the grief he had caused them both. He was afraid, no, more like grief-stricken and angst-ridden over the disappointment he anticipated on his dad's face. Thoughts of what he was about to confront seemed to be sucking the very life out of his heart. He wanted only to have done something in life that his dad was proud of. There was an assumption in him that he was going back to find the rejection he knew he deserved. Although, all he needed at this moment was security and safety found within his father's walls, the days, weeks, and months that he had been gone from home most certainly had separated his father's heart from him he thought. And honestly, he had been hardening his own heart towards his father to protect him from the emotional punishment he was about to endure. Nothing else quite made sense.

When the young man was within eye-shot distance of what used to be home, he lifted his sullen face for a moment and in the next moment lost his breath as though the wind was knocked out of him. His dad, the one whose money he blew, the one who name he smeared, the one whose advise he threw away, stood at the edge of the property with hands in pockets and a glossy-eyed smile that seemed to say 'you came home'. The anger the son had rummaged up inside against his dad was at a loss. How do you fight someone smiling at you? How should he react? What was he supposed to do? His dad started to walk toward him with a tear falling down his rough, aged face. Stunned the son couldn't move, but his dad's walk became a steady jog as reality's years of desperate prayers for his son's return fell on him. The old man quickened his pace to run as though his heart was racing to the healing of his son's broken heart. Wind whipped by the dad's face, and with every step, it shed off endless days and months of deferred hope and a sick soul. He reached his son and grabbed him into a tight and unrelenting embrace. By that time, his gray beard was soaked with the love that poured from his eyes. There were no words, but mercy fell over the son like a blanket, and love crumbled his self-hatred and misery. His entire body fell limp, and now tears rushed down from his own eyes. Suddenly that terrifying walk was the best thing he'd ever done.

Moments later, the strength from his father's love caused him to throw his own arms around his dad and in repentance grip the father who loved him. Oh! He'd walk that road a hundred times over to get the grace and mercy his father had waiting for him while he condemned himself sun up to sun down. That walk became as though nothing the instant he knew he was not his father's despise. It did not compare to the agonizing pain and desperation that exposed his heart to loneliness. It was not even as long as the blink of an eye, not when it was weighted against the acceptance he was surrounded with now.

Some people might be baffled at the reaction the father had towards the prodigal son's return, and some might not understand why this son was so ecstatic. This son was high in elation because he expected absolutely nothing from his father. What he was doing to himself in his mind is what he expected his father to offer to him and worse. He anticipated mere slavery in his father's home, if he even offered that. He might get the shell of a house, though he never expected any love or respect. But the son's heart was changed dramatically when he realized that he was worth far more than the grudging resentment his father could hold on to or the horrible disgraces he committed against himself, his father, and his father's name. When the father opened his arms to the son, he was literally opening the door of his son's heart saying 'I still love you. And I accept you.'

I think it is fascinating that when Jesus told the story of the prodigal son, his parable pictured the healing component as the father, not the mother. Today, we watch commercials where mom kisses the scraped knee, sings her kids to sleep at night, rubs their shoulders, and gives the reassuring hugs. Society says they do it all, and at times, they do seem to be everywhere all at once. Mothers have powerful roles in their children's lives, but she cannot do alone what was intended to be accomplished by dad.

More than just comfort, our soul requires a wall of strength. Somehow by way of God's intent in creation, only a man can fulfill that. Moms give love that lifts from the underside, but fathers give love that surround from the top down. She gives that light-hearted joy; he surrounds us with real, felt protection.

Mom gives me a boost of self-confidence. Dad strong hand tells me I am impenetrable. When I am my mom's, she nurtures me; when I am my dad's, he lovingly instructs me. My mom picks me up after I fell down, but what my dad is best at is stopping the fall before it starts. We all want that dad who has compassion to be these things in our life, not one who sleeps through the motions or throws away his obligation.

I remember when I was at the end of my high school years and had my wisdom teeth pulled – all four at the same time. It took a while for me to get back on my feet again. Two weeks had gone by and I was still eating applesauce and mashed potatoes. Although I had minor headaches and felt woozy off and on, I thought I was feeling minutely better. It was close to homecoming, and my mom wanted to see how I did going out shopping for a little bit. While we were out, my latent headache worsened to the point that I had to sit down and shut out the rest of the world of busy buyers. Mom knew I needed to get home, but by the time we walked through the door of our house, I couldn't take the pain anymore. It was all I could do to keep myself together, and I was ready to get back in bed. My dad came to me and asked me how I was feeling, and though I wanted to say something, I couldn't. I had been pretending I could handle the pain for too many days, and recent hours escalated everything. I just broke down crying and dropped my head face first into his chest. He laced his arms around me and let me lean into his strong frame so I could sob those quiet tears in security.

For the first time that I could remember in a long time, he just held me close and let me cry. I heard him send a gentle whisper to my mom saying they needed to get me back to the doctor. He told me to lie down and rest, and in that day I felt more protected than I had ever remembered feeling. My mom could have just as well done all the same for me, and she has. Those moments, too, were beautiful, but when my dad had done it, it meant something different. I could surrender my strength to his, and he was going to be strong for me. Dad's offering felt different than comfort. He felt like a rock I could prop up against when I was too broken to do it myself.

As it turns out I had three dry sockets, which meant the very air I breathed was touching the open nerves close to my jaw bone. Every time I took a breath, the coarse air sent my raw nerves into a frenzy and sent throbbing shocks throughout my entire head. The doctor instructed he was going to fill these open wounds that were supposed to clog up and heal themselves – kind of like a scab to a scratch. While I laid back in the chair of the exam room, he reached over me with a long thin gauze strip soaked in antibacterial ointment and stuffed the entire strand in the place where one wisdom tooth laid just 2 weeks earlier. He continued to do that for all the rest, including the fourth so that there was no question of lingering pain. In the same manner, this is what a father does. Where there are dry places in us that are open to the public, laid defenseless for further wounding, a father has the power to get in the way and fill those vulnerable and sometimes painful spots with his presence. He is that protector that says I am here, and you won't have to endure this on your own anymore. He has some sort of natural born ointment that only fathers have that do things to our hearts enabling a true healing effect. God the Father is the epitome of this healing capability. His character, transferred into our dads on earth, enable them to unknowingly perform a similar work.

God was Father to us first. He is the epitome of the fathering heart and then gave that same spirit to the men of creation. God's showmanship as a father is illustrated beautifully by his own word. The most explicit verses in scripture picturing God as Father are like a train wreck to any believer's heart. I don't mean that in a bad way. I mean that in a good way. Have you ever seen someone so full of joy by a miracle of life circumstances that they fall apart in their own tears while their heart comes undone? They look like a mess, but everything that's happening inside them is fantastically good! That's the train wreck I am talking about. That's why I portrayed the prodigal son in his own version of a mess falling apart in his father's arms. His realization of who his dad really was to him changed him forever. We all need to get to that same place of a train wreck in our own hearts so we can live like we are confident in our position as sons and daughters.

God gives us a glimpse of what the Father is for us who feel rejected, neglected, and abandoned. In Ezekiel 16, the Lord looks on a people who were forgotten and thrown away by the world.

> And say, 'This is what the Sovereign LORD says to Jerusalem: Your ancestry and birth were in the land of the Canaanites; your father was an Amorite and your mother a Hittite. On the day you were born your cord was not cut, nor were you washed with water to make you clean, nor were you rubbed with salt or wrapped in cloths. No one looked on you with pity or had compassion enough to do any of these things for you.

Rather, you were thrown out into the open field, for on
the day you were born you were despised. (3-5, NIV)

God begins by telling this people, the Israelites, where they
came from. He says 'Your ancestry . . .' Why would God begin
with the family tree? Why would God bring up the parents if
he is going to talk about the person? God shows them their
original beginnings. He wants the Israelites to know where He
brought them from. How can you appreciate the kindness of
anyone unless you really know what they have done for you?
Worship suddenly becomes so much deeper. The gratitude of
your heart sings with more clarity when you know that God
without requirement, being under no obligation, came to the
child of an Amorite and Hittite – who were idol worshipers,
an offense to His heart. He sought you in a land where He,
God, was not honored, recognized, or welcomed. He entered
into a place where He was rejected, picked you up by His own
determination and affection, and saved you.

God saw that no one cared for this people; no one else took
charge to watch over the Israelites. In fact on the day Israel was
born, she was "despised". It is difficult to imagine a baby born
in a hospital where the nurses forgot to clean him, and the
doctors forgot to go through proper protocol to make sure he
is healthy and ready to go home, let alone throw him away in a
trash can. However at the gasp of my heart, it happens nearly a
million times every year in America. Perhaps you can imagine
the man in the story of the Good Samaritan who fell among
thieves going from Jerusalem to Jericho. He was robbed, beaten
and bloodied, lying in hopelessness unable to help himself. This
is the depiction of Israel, in a sense. She was deemed as good

for nothing and left to die. So was the man. He was thrown out. What is more disturbing is the similarity that no one had compassion or pity on either helpless figure. The half dead man was passed up not only by a Levite but by a priest as well. The people who are named men of God overlooked the dying man who was laid open for rescue by anyone who had opportunity to see. Here Israel is left to herself, and "no one looked on you with pity or had compassion enough to do any of these things for you."(vs 5a, NIV)

Lots of people say 'Oh, we live in such a compassionate society!' and 'No one goes without in America.' The reality is that most of society and the world at large are unmoved by the needs and desperation of others. Or if they are moved in their heart, they stand aside and do nothing frozen in self-consciousness, afraid of what others may think or are bound in the worries of their own financial and relational stress. That is why God said "No one looked on you with pity or had compassion *enough* . . ." Sure many have some sense of compassion like an emotional tug that lasts just long enough to get back to our own affairs, but the bible says faith without actions is dead. I suggest that if we say we are moved in heart and then do not move, like the Levite or the priest, we *are* unmoved. We are without compassion. Suppose the priest in his heart had pity on the beaten man, and prayed for him with all his might as he hurried to the service he was speaking at that night. His well-abled body could have physically reached out to the man, but the priest withheld what he had. Selfish ambition over-ruled what could have been a grand expression of God's merciful love. The approaching Levite might have thought to look down and see if the man was still alive and offer him help, while lies whirled in the back of his mind of how others will accuse him of participating in such an ugly offense. Officials would question his involvement in being a contributor in the brutal attack. They might ask if he was the planned cover-up. It could look like the perfect planned finish since he was of fine reputation. He shoos the first lie away because of its ridiculousness, but while he stands there a second one arises. He sees the man as the possible criminal. The devil, that accuser of the brethren, tells the Levite that the man certainly deserved this punishment and describes a picture of how the beaten man in his own evil schemes came to an end like this. Soon he believes this criminal received exactly what God meant for him and moves on pushing out the tug in his heart. Deceit won over this man's mind of reasoning. No matter what our own personal vice, none of us on our own really have compassion enough to put faith to work, but our Creator does. And He extends it through us to others. Initially, God has compassion *enough* to extend us mercy.

His compassion is full of understanding, unlike ours. He sees the pain and depth of despondency inside our hearts and our souls. He sees the scars that line the hearts of men. Sometimes if the scene is portrayed correctly by a television commercial or told intricately by a friend, we have a measure of insight that sees a piece of the sufferer's condition. Rarely are we given the discernment to know how much trouble someone is experiencing internally without a full description before us. The essence of the pain is not usually found in broken bones, illness, or hunger alone. The pain multiplies from betrayals, denial from friends and family, lack of compassion from others, and rejection. As much as a hungry baby might feel pain in his body, the real pain is in the heart of him as he grows to understand why he was neglected the food that others readily had. He would often wonder why he was so hated. As bloodied and bruised as the beaten man was, the authentic hurt would have scared his soul if he ever woke up by himself to see a dozen more people apathetically pass by. To be invisible is a punishment unto itself. To be forgotten is an unquenchable fire. You see, the most enduring traumas are not always those in the body. Pain and anguish lay in the heart until someone comes to redeem it for love.

Looking at Israel in this context is looking at a very fragile life left unto death. No one will turn their face to see the eminent destruction unless some radical intervention is made for the man in the road or for baby Israel. Here is the hand of our Lord pursuing the broken on account of nothing else save His own compassion and mercy. God talks about His chosen people here in delicate and gentle terms. His words describe the kindness He has on a people and illustrates mercy where it is not asked for.

> Then I passed by and saw you kicking about in your blood, and as you lay there in your blood I said to you, "Live!" I made you grow like a plant of the field. You grew up and developed and became the most beautiful of jewels. (Ezekeial 16:6-7, NIV)

The Lord makes things happen by speaking them. If he wants there to be light, all He has to say is "Let there be light," and there is light. He merely puts forth words, and creations come into existence. So when God looked down on the pitiful Israel and spoke something to her, it came to be. He spoke life over the people and the people lived. However, just because it may seem like speaking is such an effortless act, God does not do it without regard to His will or desire. He first determines something to happen based upon his good character and agrees to it in Himself. Then, when He has purposed it in Himself, He speaks it into existence. We often feel compelled based on emotion, but we rarely determine something based on the goodness of God. Sometimes we even say to ourselves, 'I should do that. I know God would'. But we hesitate, we forget, or we reason ourselves out of it. It is yet God's compassion that moves in His being and draws Him to act in kindness and love. In these actions the fathering spirit arises, and what we need is not our own compassion but His.

If you have not received the revelation yet, let me take you further into one of the most familiar stories of the bible. We left off in the parable of the Good Samaritan where the man who fell to thieves is lying destitute nearing his own death. Luke 10:33-34 reads:

> But a certain Samaritan, as he journeyed, came where he was. And when he saw him, he had compassion. So he went to him and bandaged his wounds, pouring on oil and wine; and he set him on his own animal, brought him to an inn, and took care of him. (NKJ)

What is funny is that when Jesus gave the disciples this parable, it was not very much like a parable. Rather, He was retelling a story that already happened with Israel, was to continually happen between believers and dying men, and would one day happen in the fullness and glory of the Lord to all the church. The words of the prophet Ezekiel conveyed what God had done for His beloved. In the parable of the Samaritan, Jesus was merely retelling the same story with different characters on stage. You see, when Jesus was speaking this parable in the New Testament, He was not telling John and Luke and Matthew and all the rest to be like the Samaritan; He was telling the men to be like Himself. In the story of Israel, God is the Samaritan figure. He had already done it, and the story had already been told many hundred years ago. He, God, had found Israel lying helpless and abandoned, and He was moved in His heart to take her in. This is exactly what the character of the Samaritan did for the man. This was more like a heart compelling testimony than a fictitious fable for Jesus to tell, rekindling His own memories of bringing a beloved nation from depravity to fullness. The Father's heart was the living component that reached out to his future children.

What is more, God does not stop at mere rescue. You see, the Samaritan pays the inn keeper to watch over the beaten man, and he promises to come back and bring more money to pay for any expenses that are necessary for his recovery. He desires and puts forth the effort to nurse this man back to life again, at all costs. Let's see what God was really illustrating in Ezekiel when he was painting this picture with Israel.

> "I bathed you with water and washed the blood from you and put ointments on you. I clothed you with an embroidered dress and put leather sandals on you. I dressed you in fine linen and covered you with costly garments. I adorned you with jewelry: I put bracelets on your arms and a necklace around your neck, and I put a ring on your nose, earrings on your ears and a beautiful crown on your head. So you were adorned with gold and silver; your clothes

were of fine linen and costly fabric and embroidered cloth. Your food was fine flour, honey and olive oil. You became very beautiful and rose to be a queen. And your fame spread among the nations on account of your beauty, because the splendor I had given you made your beauty perfect, declares the Sovereign LORD. (Ezekiel 16:9-14, NIV)

God did not just nurse Israel to health but he flourished her to a most magnificent existence, a glory that only God can bestow. Although God so longs for us to move in His mercy, and it is one of the wonderful revelations of the story of the Good Samaritan, it is not where he finishes His work. Like He did for Israel, God wants to raise us up to high places and give us the best gifts as a father would. He doesn't want us to have just enough, He is a God of more than enough. And to put it plainly, a woman doesn't need jewelry or crowns or fine linen to have good health. Nor does anyone need fame to survive. But these things are His to give us, and everything that is His, He gives freely. You see, He didn't merely raise Israel, He cherished her. In the verses between her destitution as an outcast and riches as a queen is this, "I made you thrive like a plant in the field; and you grew, matured, and became very beautiful . . . Yes, I swore an oath to you and entered into a covenant with you, and you became Mine," says the Lord GOD." (Ezekiel 16:7,8, NKJ) God truly fathered Israel and was able to because in reality He had adopted her.

God had to make Israel his personal interest. He took her in, and she became His total responsibility. He put that decision on His own head. She became His burden and His delight. He made her His own because only one that is His would receive all that He has to offer. Only a Father or a husband would say "you became mine". God has inside of Himself the desire to bring us into His own house, to say that everything He has is ours. He could sit and watch us from a distance, but then how could he rescue when that requires getting in the mess? God says that His arm is not too short to save us for a reason. He is our Father, like the daddy that keeps you from crossing the street when you are not supposed to and picks you up off the concrete when you have fallen off your bike and skinned your knees. He is the daddy that that takes his run-away child back into His house and lifts up our defeated and broken hearts with His soft words and a strong chest.

The father's healing touch is the very point of all God's works in the earth today and a thousand years ago and two thousand years ago and so on and so on. He desires restoration, relationship, covenant - that everlasting "yes" that binds His heart and yours together as one. God is always trying to get us back in perfect relationship with Him. That is his ultimate goal. But there is a wide gap that separates the Father from us. Romans 3:23 says that we have all sinned, meaning without God there is no denying our likeness to the enemy who has eternal sin. We are children born into sin and of this world. Spiritually we are born into a fatherless existence, and we have no protection. We are, by way of nature, born into orphanhood. If we had to claim any father, it would be the very one who wants to destroy us. Without steady and unshifting love constantly at our hearts, the rebellion of sin is what we know. Sin is what we are affiliated with. It isn't just what we do, but it is what we are friends with and what we accept in others, in work, and in all systems of life. It infiltrates everything. And if we are born to sin and born to this world, then the essence of our need is a new origin.

God chooses his love as our new place of beginning. He picks us up like He did Israel and puts in His house all of those who agree to be taken in. He offers to love us with a real, rich love. This selfless action is His initiation. God says himself in Ephesians 4:6 that there is one God and Father of all. We each have a unique father on earth, but we are all called ultimately to the same Father of a higher order. All men's and women's satisfaction is met in one God. This is a Father we must choose to have though. A transaction has to take place. We must be adopted from fatherlessness. God seeks to make us children of Himself, of the promise, and of heaven. *He* wants to infiltrate our life. We can receive that fatherly healing ointment only when we agree to be his child. A daddy cannot be a daddy unless he first calls us his son or daughter, and God turns to us and asks, 'Can I call you my child?' To have the one Father of guidance, He has to adopt us that He may speak into our lives and protect us. This transaction empties us of anything else, including the sin that we may give ruling power over our life, and it gives complete power to a new guardian, to one Father.

Consider the apostle Paul. God called Paul to be his child. Paul was born of Jewish descent, and he was a radical Jew defending his faith by slaughtering Christians in every opportunity. But in that act, while Paul was committing murder zealously for the religious faith he knew, he was not yet in God or partaking as a child of God. That is because he didn't yet *know* God and didn't receive Him. As soon as God found Paul, he responded with a pleading yes! There are physical children of Abraham, Isaac and Jacob. There are physical children of Israel. But not all of those are children of God. And certainly none of the Gentiles will ever be God's children unless they come to know the one true God. It is only the ones that say yes. The Creator of our soul is calling us to be His children. When we hear the call and answer it is when something happens. At that moment, we have the life changing opportunity to let His best be our rest as we give up all our strife to Him. He seeks to have those who are living now in spiritual death. He is seeking the sick, the bound, and the broken. Our God actively desires to be in relationship with us all, whether we are currently His or not. He is a Father-God, and longs to see us fathered. The crucial key is a living relationship. The God-shaped hole in us all can only be filled by knowing God as the Father.

He is bringing people into his house and making their problems His own, and being the caretaker to all of them. He is the one who has compassion on those who are on their back. His mercy is what reaches down and forms love inside us and says "You are mine." God is not a meticulous, condescending, anger-stricken, rule-bullying stickler. The mystery of being His is found in the warmth of His arms and in His tender affections. It is a place you want to be when you need to be comforted or when you want to rejoice. Ultimately, the Father's house is the place you want to live. The result of being God's is not to live in hindrance but in freedom.

For all of those who received a bad fathering experience, know that a father is meant to be the source of protection in our natural life, at least for a time. No one should have to find a place of protection from their father. Of course, I am not making any references to well made corrections and godly discipline from parents. What I am saying is that our fathers should be the place we actually desire to run to. God purposefully created everything in such an order so that earthly fathers would be an example of His Fatherhood. He is our permanent protection. He is our safe place. And if your home or your earthly father did not render for you a safe place in His heart or create that with his presence, then it was not what God intended. God intends to be the place (and sometimes is the only place) where you feel safe. He wants you to be truly fathered, and there is still time for you to experience His fatherly affections now.

As we search out relationship with the Heavenly Father, we are given the capacity to take on the same love and character for our children's benefit. Randy Bohlender of the Zoe Foundation in Kansas City has an amazing work raising money and awareness for adoption through his ministry. He and his wife, Kelsey, also split their time as intercessory missionaries at the International House of Prayer and serve on leadership for TheCall. In a teaching entitled Finding Adoption in the Prayer Movement, Randy intricately linked the heart of prayer and love for Jesus with the power of adoption through the Father's heart. He said, "So when you ask me how does intimacy with Jesus lead you to take action in children, I say, 'How can you claim intimacy without developing a heart to emulate the way he found you?'" If Jesus came to display the affections of the Father toward us, and if the Father had done all these things on our behalf, taking us in when we were nothing but a helpless child crying out in our own blood, and if we truly understood the lengths he took to save us, we would be so undone in this compassion that we would pour out the Father's heart on the children in our community without hesitation. What is more, we would be compelled to be like Him, doing for others what He did for us.

We would in effect walk out what Christians really are, little christs, or more appropriately be the fathers to lost children like God is a Father to us.

Psalm 103:13 says, "The Lord has loving-pity on those who fear Him, as a father has loving-pity on his children." (NLV) This scripture gives an example to humans of who God is, but the way it is written is merely done for the benefit of our understanding. It describes God in terms of what we understand: fathers. If we zoom our perspectives out, we will see the greater universal reality in the scripture - that earthly fathers are an example of who God is. It is a man's inherit born trait and God-given destiny to grow into the fullness of a loving father. In similar words of Randy Bohlender, men were made in like fashion of God to "emulate" the very pinnacle of what He is for us. If being in the Lord's manifest presence is heaven and the opposite is hell, then without men standing in their role as compassionate fathers, children turn to the orphan spirit, and what we have is hell on earth.

One father not fulfilling his duty makes room for hell in his home. A nation of fathers not fulfilling their role establishes this bondage from sea to shining sea. The atmosphere of a nation changes when the role of this one entity disappears. In thirty years time, from 1980 to 2008, single parent homes has grown by well over 4 million children, and you can guess that the vast majority of them are led by mothers (U.S. Bureau of Labor Statistics). In 1980 approximately 20% of children lived in single parent households. In 2010, that number grew to over one third of our nation's child population at 34% (Ann E. Casey Foundation). If these numbers continue to climb, it will take less than one generation's time before the majority, not a minority, of our children are found raised in single parent homes. This living condition will become the norm. What does that mean for the infiltration of loneliness? It would have great reign in our nation by sheer numbers. What does that mean for the expansion of God's kingdom of love? It will slowly dissipate being quenched by the fire of Satan's orphan rule. If our fathers do not arise now, the scars in this land may be too brutal for recovery in our children's lives, and humanity will be left waiting on a godly man to rise up in their children's lives. Why wait on another generation, when the charge begins with you?

The bible says, "Everyone who believes that Jesus is the Christ is born of God, and everyone who loves the father loves his child as well" (1 John 1:5, NIV). The immediate context of this verse is speaking about Christ. He is the begotten Son of God, and if we love God the Father, we are found loving Christ. The wider context of this verse demands that we as believers in the faith must also be found as lovers of everyone who is a child of God. While God is setting destinies for new lives that come into the world day after day, he calls out the fathers in the earth to live out their faith and love them as he has required. He says in the last part of that verse that we must love "his child as well." I suppose less than a demand, it is more of a fruit. If you love the Father, the verse beckons then without question you will love his child in action too. Did not Christ say whatever we do to the least of these we do to Him? (Matthew 25:40) Loving a child as a son is loving the Son who in the trinity became your Father. We touch God when we love people.

Cindy Jacobs, a leader in intercession ministry worldwide and author of a number of highly powerful and influential works, writes in her 2007 book Reformation Manifesto:

God is giving us, His Church, the chance to redeem ourselves by rescuing the next generation waiting to be born through our willingness to open our homes and adopt. With all my heart I know that God is going to require members of churches who think that they are beyond the point of wanting to raise a child to be willing to adopt children others planned to abort. We need to prove not only through word, but through deed, that we want to marry righteousness with justice in our land. (Pg 204)

It is by compassion enough that we can marry our righteousness as priests and Levites with the justice of the Samaritan. If we say we are godly men and women and yet do not follow him, how can we claim God at all? Furthermore, how can God claim us as His if we don't participate in any of his likeness? I reason we must do exactly as Cindy and Randy have proposed.

CHAPTER

Grafted into Identity

6

Way back in the sticks of some small, obscure town in Texas where income levels are well below average and everything appears quaint, an unexpected miracle had emerged in the late 90s that became a national phenomenon. Donna Martin, a pastor's wife in that small town, heard God speak to her one day. In the midst of a troubling time in her life, God asked her to give of herself when it felt like she did not have the strength to hold her own head up. She had just lost her beloved mother. God was asking her to adopt children. Though there were some great hesitations, she took a step forward in faith and began that journey. As she and her husband obeyed the call, it fell swiftly on the hearts of their friends and congregation members as though the same call was spreading in contagion into the heart of the town. What resulted was a 200 member church adopting 72 children from the foster care system. The icing on the miracle was that not one parent released their adopted child back into the system. Not one child was given up on nor rejected

DENISE BUCKBINDER GANUCHEAU

no matter how taxing or how much endurance was required for the full transformation of that child in their new home.

Donna's sister, Diann, actually became the first to adopt in the small town of Possum Trot, Texas. She had heard Donna talk about this heart pull from the Lord and decided to join her in the pursuit. In Pastor W.C. Martin's book, Small Town Big Miracle, he tells a piece of Diann's story with her recently adopted four-year-old son. She hadn't had him in her home long and though he was quite reserved in nature, she had already learned to love him.

> Diann had never seen him cry. But one evening, she peeked into Nino's bedroom and saw tears streaming down his cheeks. "What's wrong?" she asked. He choked up. "I wanna go back home," he said.
>
> She stood there for a moment. With all she could muster from within, she said with a warm but confident love, "I'm your mama now." He didn't say anything. She hugged Nino and told him it would be okay. As time went on, he came to understand. And he came to know her as his "Mama".
>
> One day, sometime later, he looked up at Diann with his little brows frowning. "Mama," he said, "why did you wait so long to come and get me?" Tears filled her eyes. "Well," she answered, "it took me all that time to find you." And she picked him up and just held him.

It is only natural that one father and mother raise their own child, and another raise theirs. That is the way creation was made. But what is contrary to that nature is when one mother and father take in a child of another family. The seemingly right thing would be to have the original parents take care and raise their own birth child. No one should give up their child willingly, give away such a responsibility, or trample such a treasure. But in a world where imperfections crush the possibility of a painless and unflawed life, children find themselves without a family, without guardians, and without protection for their vulnerable hearts all too often. God enters the scene and sees this problematic situation. He says that He knows how He created life to be, but He must make an amendment for this awkward and torn situation. In His mercy, He reaches across the chasm of impossibility through His Son and says 'I am going to graft you into my family'.

Little Nino experienced that kind of grafting. Diann reached across the chasm of abuse and loneliness to offer this little boy another chance at love and acceptance. Indeed, Nino had enjoyed the tangibles of his new home as well. He was given a calm and consistent atmosphere with the provisions his little body required and desired, but tears and troubling emotions held on to him until he learned to embrace his new mom with his heart. He had to come to know the relationship he could have with his caretaker to really enjoy the full life of that home. Her groceries and his new bedroom couldn't console his soul. He needed to be grafted into the family. Likewise, in order for us to enter the fullness of God's family, we must be grafted into the heart of God just as much as we are grafted into the benefits of God. Enjoying what God gave us without enjoying the relationship he has offered us is only part of His plan.

Paul says that ". . . you were cut out of an olive tree that is wild by nature, and contrary to nature were grafted into a cultivated olive tree . . ." (Romans 11:24, NKJ). God is a God of order, and we came from what was unorderly – the chaos of this world. He chose us, having not been born of Him, to come and live in Him. And what is most astounding is that Paul uses the word "contrary". It is contrary to nature that we have a place with God and in God. It is contrary to the way everything was formed that we have rights to go boldly before the throne of grace. It is contrary to many standards that we are able to know God. It is contrary to nature that an unknown child be loved by another willing and loving parent. Because God broke the rules to rescue us; we have the capability to go against nature and rescue others.

The word used for graft in the Greek here is *egkentrizō* which is derived from two words. The first word, en, is a preposition that denotes a fixed position (E-Sword). The second word, kentron, means a point or a sting (E-Sword). I like to look at it this way: God has put us in a fixed position pointed in Him. We are grafted into the vine, pointed into the trinity, purposely fixed toward him. Graft as defined by the English language is described as 'a shoot or bud of one plant or tree inserted or to be inserted into the stem or trunk of another, where it continues to grow, becoming a permanent part' and 'a joining of one thing to another' (Neufeldt, pg 585). Nino couldn't exist merely as a traveling visitor in Diann's home, neither could he be a lifelong consumer. These were not the intentions of Diann's actions. He had to see himself as a permanent part of her family. God saw us where we were and decided He would be our Father, and then joined us to Himself. We become a permanent part of Him, and He becomes a permanent part of us. God wants us to abide in Him, and He will abide in us. When our Father says that He will never leave us or forsake us, He means us to accept Him as a permanent figure in our life. He is not going to get us through our senior year of school then drop us off at college and say "See ya! Good luck!" He has made us one with him. Jesus said He and the Father are one (John 10:30). He also said, "that they all may be one, as You, Father, are in Me, and I in You; that they also may be one in Us" (John 17:21, NKJ).

When our hearts attach fully to God, a heart transplant takes place and it changes the way we look at ourselves. Just like Diann's adopted son, little Nino, had to find out who his new "Mama" was and then had to accept that new reality, we too go through the same process with God. Nino's conclusion to the matter, though, was not one that remained external to his life, but to him a new mother meant he had a new identity. His love for her, his heart position which became fixed toward her, enabled him to become someone completely different than his past home had made possible.

My pastor, Jim Hennessy, said on Father's Day morning in 2011 about the role of a father, "[Fathers] announce the identity of their children through their strength and through their stories. They identify the potential." This is a bold and perhaps frightening statement for men to hear because suddenly it requires another level of responsibility, but it also recognizes the power fathers are embodied with. To have affect and influence over any human is weighty in the eyes of the Lord. What we do with it will be a witness for or against us. God, however, did not hesitate to pass out this gift to men. When little children cannot quite conceive of an omni-everything God, fathers represent a tangible picture of where they came from. It's like a baby animal who looks at its mother for the first time when their eyes have opened, and in that instant they know they are of that particular make-up. What a child sees in their father is what their heart wears as their identity badge. Their soul says, "This is who I am." No child can know his identity without identifying his father. And through time, our own soul looks up to God in clearer and clearer vision and says, "This is who I am in the likeness of." Where we graft in is where we find our reflection.

My husband and I were in the car one day headed out to Wednesday night church discussing fathers and their roles. Jonathan pointed out an interesting scenario in Genesis. Adam was given the domain by God to name all the animals in the earth, and once it was established that none of those were a viable partner for him, God created woman. What we notice here is that again God gave Adam authority to name this new helper. From these beginnings, Adam used his right to give identities to all created animals and second, to a created human. Identity comes from man because God in heaven endowed him with such power. It was established in the very beginning, and God has not recanted. Because males are in the naming business, it is in essence the gift of the father to give identity to their children.

As I looked into this recorded story I found that Adam named his wife both 'woman' as a general concept of her identity in Genesis 2:23 and gave her individuality in the specific name Eve in Genesis 3:20. Her husband wove her identity in its origination – woman meaning that she came from man, and he incorporated her identity in her destiny as the bearer of life. Eve means life or living. Amazingly, identities often speak two things: what we come from and what we are destined for. To put it simply, it is our origination and our purpose, our past and our future. Woman was not slighted in this process. Her gift is to bear life and be a mother to the living, something that man has no capacity to do. Once that life is brought forth, the father's gift is to name the child or give an identity that will remain with him.

Of course mothers and fathers often decide on names together in this day and age, but consider our history in the word. God told Zechariah, not Elizabeth, the name of his son, and in turn Zechariah as father was the one to give it. Even after he questioned the angel of the Lord and endured some months of chastisement, the right to name his child, John, was still given to him. The name John in its original Hebrew means 'Yahweh is gracious'. This young child grew up to become John the Baptist, the voice calling out in the desert as prophesied by Isaiah. He was making straight paths for the coming of the Messiah in the Spirit of Elijah. He proclaimed the graciousness of God as a forerunner of God's ultimate love gift to us. Uniquely, God was announcing the destiny of John the Baptist when he 'announced', as Jim Hennessy said, the name of the man. Inside John's name was his destiny. Yet the last right to announce the name came to Zechariah. He was to pass the baton of the name John to the world.

In a parallel occurrence, God told Joseph, not Mary, his son would be called Jesus. Jesus' name comes from a shortened version of another Hebrew name, Joshua. The translation of the two is 'Yahweh is salvation'. Isn't that exactly what Jesus is, our salvation? The identity of this life once again was announced in the name. It is who He was and what He came to do. It is the essence of His fulfillment in His earthly life and forever. The Lord, who had already previously given the authority of naming to men, passed this information along to the faithful man in Jesus' life. God could have very plainly told the women in each scenario the names, but as Father of all, He passed on the children's' names to their earthly fathers as witness of the continued authority of man to give identity. I don't want to focus too much on how we name our children today, even though I think that is an important process. I used that demonstration to make evidence for the connection between fathers and identity. Every human's identity is built intricately in the mixture of three components: position, power, and potential. Potential is the last and the most significant of the three because it is the sum or maybe even the product of the first two. To use Jim Hennessy's words again, fathers "identify the potential" within us. Our identity is directly linked to our potential, and our potential is formed by the person we accept as our dad.

The first element is position, but don't get caught up in the concept of your position. That's not what we're talking about here. I'm talking about the position of your father. And his position is not so much what he is or where he is placed as much as it is the position to which he is aimed at and facing. It's more like where he is grafted. This is what affects the identity of his child. I know, you're asking me what I mean. Let's bring out some examples. A father's position is less about what job he has and more about how he does it. Man's position is less about what he has achieved and more about what he has overcome to achieve it. It's less about how many friends he has and more about what kind of friendships he builds and protects. A man who is loyal on the job has a position of consistency and high work ethic. A dad who overcomes is poised with perseverance, dignity, and often humility. A man who cherishes his friends and family is positioned with genuine love. The physical things in life including items like titles and wealth can be held in the hand, and those are the things that are evident to any onlooker. But these don't really dictate his position. They are not *who* he is. They are merely what he *has*. True position recognizes what the man is when everything is stripped away from him. If I take all the rich man's cash, investments, and wealth, is he still rich in soul? What do his eyes tell you? This is essence. This is his position.

It is more like an action than a noun. You can think of it as being positioned or poised. It is a continual working, always and constantly focused toward something else. It is a lifestyle that can only be expressed or upheld by the living. It is not a stagnant adjective, i.e. the china is gold or the statue is tall. Neither is it a level achieved where a person can lay down and halt further pursuit, i.e. landing an executive job or a high paying salary. Instead position is what creates such an achievement. This is much different from our normal understanding. Personal physical gain is never our end. Instead the position of a man is something that is persistent, something that perseveres. James says so. "Let perseverance finish its work so that you may be mature and complete, not lacking anything." (James 1:4, NIV) He doesn't say 'having finances and wealth not lacking anything'. If we had much in finances yet nothing else, we would be lacking everything. What an awful position to be in.

When it comes to God's position, we know that the bible says He is love. We also know that He is an omnipotent God and cannot be stripped of anything right? - Except when he stripped himself of His throne and became fully human. He was stripped from heaven and walked among the filth of sin; although our God was still positioned as holy and completely righteous. He was stripped of all his glory according to the human eye, and we thought him no different than the common man. But he displayed His power by performing an unending list of miracles, and glory ensued. He was stripped of the right to be untouchable and became vulnerable to our touch, yet when men beat him he poured out mercy on them. I could go on, but you see how God displayed who He was through Jesus. His position was evident to all. This position was so true of the essence of God that Jesus said anyone who had seen Jesus had seen the Father. The position of God is the direction He is facing in love. In essence, the position of a man boils down to his character. It is the one thing you cannot strip from him. They stripped all from Jesus, but in the end while he hung on a cross, He could not be stripped of the character of God.

Assuming that our identity lies somehow in the identity of our father, his position of character is going to greatly influence who we think we are or who we should be. How many children beam when they get to tell their school friends what their dads do for work on show-and-tell day? Why are they so excited? Because when their father's work is great it reflects greatness in them. The subconscious mental capacity of the heart goes something like this, "My father is not only capable of accomplishing this, he does accomplish it! And that means I can do that or more someday." The label of the father is transferable to the child. On the other hand, a child who is ashamed of his father does not even want to recognize his existence. A father who is in prison, who made no effort to change the lifestyle that got him there, and who never spent time with his son in the first place is an embarrassment to anyone. Why? If this were your father, how would it affect you? Bringing up your father's life would only invite slanderous insults of where you might end up. If the child chooses not to talk about him, then he does not have to face his father's failure and the subsequent thoughts that his own failure is all too often just around the corner. In the battlefield of the mind, it's hard to rise above your own bloodline. In the same sense, especially during our innocent years, it is hard to imagine that we can fail if we have a bright and successful one.

Position tells us where our fathers can go, not just where they currently are. It is both the end result and also the means for gain in the realm of the physical. Position also indirectly tells their offspring where they can go. It holds a certain amount of ruling in their life and the next. Power is the natural following point in identity. The power of our fathers are directly enabled by the course they are positioned. A father who loves all people and has a loving character has the power to pour that love into his wife and children and ultimately transform them with it for the better. The power I mean here is not just to make wealth or move mountains; although these are great powers bestowed on men and given by our God. Those things are indeed great power, and I want to acknowledge that. But I want to hone down on a very specific kind of power. That is the power to influence.

A father is innately bestowed with the gift to affect his child's heart with either honor or destruction. He cannot walk away from or give up this power. Even if he never meets his child, the influence of what he has not done greatly moves his child's experience and understanding of self. Everything the father does, good or bad, is being written on his child's heart and in his memory. The key factor that makes the direction of this influence is his position in terms of character. The question is not 'Does the father have power to influence his child?' but

'With his God-given influence, how does he steer the future of his child?' Will a father build up his son or daughter or will he destroy their heart, their joy, and their self-esteem? That is often mightily based in what kind of character he has. The position or character of a father often determines what his power will wield in the children he brings to life.

I recently read an article about a father and son team who came together to create a unique way to self publish. The father had fiction stories he wanted to get out, and the grown son had some novel insights on how to work the realm of social media. Together they planned to release audio versions of the father's book chapter by chapter over time in order to engage the listener - much like a weekly television series might keep the audience captive until the following show. As I read the article, their relationship slowly unwrapped. It is unique enough that we see fathers and sons working together on projects let alone in professional business, but their relationship seemed to flourish well beyond industry. The father, Andrew, showed such respect for his son's inventive ideas and technological aid to what he admitted was not his strength. His quotes had a graciousness about them, and I suppose it took humility to admit that his son understood an entire arena that he did not even dare enter. The son revealed even more. "Our family spent a lot of time without a television," Todd Lovato said. "It was all about sitting around and a lot of talking. That's how I feel when I listen to the podcasts. It brings me back to the campfires" (Quintana). I can almost see the gazing admiration in Todd's eye as he reminisces about his childhood when his father would tell long awaited stories. They almost immediately bring warmth to the heart. Todd's comments reciprocated the feeling of respect towards his dad. His dedication to work with him seems to tell of a true love he has for him.

Andrew and Todd have a tremendous relationship. This little article casting light into a small segment of a father and son's life reveals what one generation had done so positively to affect the next. For starters, Andrew's character is revealed. We might have to read between the lines to get it, but I found out that Andrew is gracious, humble, and respectful especially toward his son. True, while growing up Todd did not have a television, which means Andrew probably didn't make a lot of money. But it's not what Andrew had in his hands that influenced his son. It is where his character was positioned. Although we cannot see this part of their life, I would guess this father did some encouraging for his son's self-esteem and investing in his future career. Andrew was positioned with an abundance of positive love and moral, and because of that, he was able to positively influence his son Todd. With this power, he may have been the foremost role model empowering Todd to become the successful and whole person he is today. That influence is easily seen in the memories Todd has of his father. Those happy recollections are ingrained in Todd's mind and probably on his heart. This son has not forgotten those long ago moments his father had used to invest in him. They are still alive in Todd as a grown man perhaps some twenty years later. This is the power of influence, and that brings us to the third point: Potential.

Potential has to do with all the abilities inside us and the connected possibilities of our future. Potential addresses the destiny of a person and the realization of it. It's the question that asks 'what is my destiny?' Potential says whether you have a destiny, and much more so, whether you can accomplish it.

Potential could be revealed in the subconscious thoughts of your mind that determine most all your life's decisions. Do you really believe you can graduate from college? If not, then you probably didn't give it much try when you were there or you just didn't go. Do you really think you are a good friend to others worthy of deep relationships? Do you believe others like you for you? The ways you respond to these types of subconscious questions drive your actions. We form these concepts about ourselves by looking back on the predecessors of our life – mom, and even weightier dad.

While Todd could have been crushed as a child by a tyrant of father or left abandoned by a man who never told him he could excel in anything, this obviously was not his situation. But had it been, Todd could very well have grown up another person, perhaps too timid to try anything or too mean and abusive to have any real relationships. He could have had a different outlook on life seeing it only as a cruel game for killing dreams or an impossible mess to understand and so never daring to venture out in what his heart desired. These character changes would likely have given Todd a different future entirely. He would have made decisions based on those other things he believed. His decisions, of course, carve out his unique path of life. Yet even though he could have experienced a more destitute outlook on himself and life, it doesn't mean that was what he was made to become or how he was made to operate. Quite the contrary, Todd has a plan marked over his life regardless of the offenders that are empowered to steer him away from it. The plan is always the same. God wrote it, and because He never changes the plan never does.

Think of potential as a ball of energy inside a child. He can either choose to believe in that innate potential that is already inside him, or he can choose to dismiss it. If he dismisses it, he squelches the life of the fire. It doesn't get put out because God's plan is never demolished, but in the eyes of the child, it is nearly dead. The faith that child has in his potential will cause that life of potential inside him to rise and fall like a light with a sliding switch that smoothly dims or brightens at the turn of a hand. What affects the increase or decrease of a child's belief in himself? It is how he or she answers the raw question: Who am I? The immediate answer comes to a small child through the face of their father. I gave scenarios of children looking to their father and drawing positive or negative self-esteems a few pages back. A child is only going to draw self-esteem and self-worth from something that has great power over determining who they are. 'So a father determines who his child is?' you ask sardonically. My answer, no. But the child thinks so. Every living thing looks to where it came from and uses that assessment to determine where it is going. Does your favorite pet dog think he is human because you raised him from a pup? I bet he wants to sit at the table and eat human food with you. He wants to ride in the front seat of the car with the window rolled down.

I'm sure you've heard the statistics of abused sons who become abusive. Or take for instance, alcoholics or addicts who were sons of addicts. Perhaps you would want to consider the incarceration rate of men whose father's were incarcerated . . . or just absent from their lives. No, the rate isn't one hundred percent nor is it even half in most cases. But it is many times multiplied from sons whose fathers did none of these things. The increase in rate is dramatic. I'm sure none of these men or women wanted to become what their father was, and I'm even surer they wouldn't admit that they ever believed they'd end up in the same spot. In fact their true God given potential says they have a much higher purpose. But deep down in their heart, in the back of their mind, when they saw their father their hope for their personal destiny and potential wilted. It was as if their faith was momentarily dimmed and subsequent thoughts capped their future to the things they saw their fathers become.

When a child looks at his father, whether he admits it or rejects it, something inside him says that's my identity. It may be a joy or it may be the doom that haunts them. The position of the father coupled with his innate power to influence his child facilitates the answer to the child's question of identity. A failed father makes for a child who believes he is a failure who then has complete diminished faith in his own potential to be the best of whatever his dreams entail. A loving father makes for a child who believes he is loving and loves others. He has an increased faith in his own potential to shoot for the stars because all that love has built him up in faith.

Potential begs the question: Where are you going? Are you going to the ultimate place God has for you? Or are you milling about in circles aimlessly because you don't believe in yourself? Or are you killing off the very pieces of your heart that tell you you can do it, destroying the life God planned for you? We have to back up a little farther to get the big picture here. Once again, this item is more about the son's heart then his current state. The previous topics, position and power, are of the father's nature. This last item, potential, is what those two birth in the son or daughter. The position plus the power of the father equals the surety of their son's and daughter's potential. Sure I know that there are many a child who arise out of the ashes of a dark past or a terrible home life or even out of fatherlessness. But these stories do not happen without someone somewhere in their life taking the position of a father, even if for only one conversation, one sentence, or one far away speech to a crowd. These moments, short relationships, or lifelong mentors override and then rewrite the position and power their birth father once held if the child allows it.

If this is possible, we have to ask, can a good father figure replace a bad father figure in every destructive situation to a son or daughter? The answer - yes, but only if the child is willing to graft into that new source. Emotionally, relationally, and spiritually speaking, why not? People form new relationships all the time. It wouldn't be an easy one to accomplish, but we didn't ask about ease. We just asked if it is possible. The hard part is finding good fathers, good men to step in, or bad fathers who are willing to change. Many processes in the child have to take place once a new relationship is initiated, and it isn't easy on the child. It takes time, years, to fully accept and become like your new dad. There is a man's story in the bible about such aspects of change in the process of finding that new potential.

In Genesis, God became Father to Abraham and gave him a new identity. The very first recording of God communicating with Abram, He tells him to get up leave his whole family, father and mother included, and go some other place that He is going to give him. "The Lord had said to Abram, "Go from your country, your people and your father's household to the land I will show you" (Genesis 12:1, NIV). If we just stop right there, we see that God made Abraham an orphan first. Abraham had to know before he followed God that God was his life source.

If Abraham already had a type of life source, meaning his parents and his familiar way of doing life, he may have never developed full dependence on God as a small child does towards his father. If a child is going to be adopted, don't they first have to be parentless? An enticing aspect of this man's story is that Abraham was not his original name. God renamed Abram, the name his earthly parents gave to him. "No longer will you be called Abram; your name will be Abraham, for I have made you a father of many nations" (Genesis 17:5, NIV). God was able to rename this man because He very decidedly made Abraham His own son by adoption. No one else had that right in Abram's life. Only Abram's father had that power, and Abram had submitted to a new father in heaven. If you go down the street, pick up a kid at a foster home or the hospital, and decide to adopt him, you go through all the paperwork and the previous parents relinquish all rights to the child, guess what happens? The child gets your name. Hello! What a revelation. God renamed Abraham like a new parent renames their adopted child because now God is saying "you are mine". In addition to that, if you adopt a child at birth, not only do they get your last name but you get to pick out a first name for them. You have full authority to establish what the child will be called from that point forward. This is what is in God's mind for his sons and daughters.

Abraham was also given a grandiose promise of an inheritance that the descendants of his bloodline would receive the Promised Land and that his descendants would be like the stars in the sky. Who gives inheritances to men, except a father? Tradition all over the world for thousands upon thousands of years says that the children inherit the property of their fathers. Well, God owns all the land on planet earth (Lev. 25:23). God says that all the gold and all the silver are his (Haggai 2:8). In Psalm 50:10-11(NIV) God says "every animal of the forest is mine, and the cattle on a thousand hills . . . every bird in the mountains . . . and the insects in the fields are mine." In verse 12 God says, "For the world is mine, and all that is in it." Basically, if there was anyone who owned everything, it is none other than the Creator. Abraham was inheriting what his new Father already owned. (That's not to say Abraham was receiving everything in God's pocket book, but what Abraham did receive was already in the pocket book.) The only way God could give Abraham an inheritance is that He first owned all He would give him. If God doesn't own it, then He can't give it. Fortunately for Abraham, God owns everything.

Abraham was plucked out of his own family and made an orphan. He was given a new name and the promise of an inheritance by God because God had adopted him into his family. In picture terms, God took a wild olive shoot named Abram and said 'I want to graft you into Me'. Paul said in Romans ". . . you, though a wild olive shoot, have been grafted in among the others and now share in the nourishing sap from the olive root . . ." (Romans 11:17, NIV). We were a wild man, woman, or child, needing to be subdued by the extravagance of God's love, and He willingly picked you up and apportioned you into His very being. You didn't deserve to come close to Him. The wild olive shoot knew nothing of the nourishing olive root. In like manner before his adoption, the little boy Nino whose story is in the beginning of this chapter knew nothing of Diann. But Diann was to him the very possibility of a new and loving life. If she hadn't stepped in, who would have?

We were all lost, homeless, a wild olive shoot doing our own thing, going our own way. But if you want to be saved you are automatically and instantaneously fathered. He now calls you His own, and you can lean on Him for everything from here to Kingdom come, literally! God is a God of adoption. And adoption is not this side note thing over here that glues two of the five hundred pieces of doctrine together. I am saying that adoption is it. It is the entire point of your existence. It is the entire point of the gospel. It is the entire point of Jesus, and it is the opposite of sin's costly entanglement. It is God's mercy and grace. It is what He preached from the beginning. It is by nature His way, though unnatural by the earthly systems He first created.

Doug Stringer wrote a book called Who's Your Daddy Now? Inside he talks about the plights of fatherlessness and the current situation in our society today. He strikes a chord when he discusses the responsibility we have to live out the revelation of God's love we have been given.

> We have a responsibility to a generation – statistically proven to be fatherless – looking for spiritual fathers. We must adopt this orphaned generation and direct them toward our Heavenly Father, who desires to seal them with His Spirit of Adoption.
>
> At the same time, many in my generation don't know how to be good fathers – including me. But those who are desperate for fathers are not expecting us to know how, but to be willing. (Stringer 70)

CHAPTER

7

Whose Orphan is He?

Today in America federal and state governments have in place foster care programs for the abused, neglected, and homeless children of our country. It is the instituted place of harbor for the forgotten and refused. The history behind the campaign begins more like a heartfelt grass roots ministry for social justice. A gentleman by the name of Charles Loring Brace arrived in New York to complete his training in seminary in the 1850s. Without the anticipation of anything but completing his schooling, his eyes were filled the horrific scene of an estimated 30,000 homeless children roaming the streets in New York City. The orphans sold small items to get very little money and would band together in gangs to protect themselves. Brace wanted to see these children have a fair start in the hopeful arms of Christian parents away from the city of their early demise. So with great conviction, he brought together The Children's Aid Society and The New York Foundling Hospital to back up efforts to offer these children to a more promising life. They were placed on trains and sent to the west in rural areas where farmers would come out to meet the young children, pick one, and take him or her home. The system rapidly became known as the *orphan train*. These fruitful initiatives of the ambitious Mr. Brace have been considered the beginning of America's foster care system.

As many as 200,000 children were sent on the orphan trains to new beginnings. Some children ended up in good homes and some ended up in homes where the families saw them as little more than free labor. The plight is that while some were rescued, others were sent to the same situation of abuse and neglect hundreds of miles away from New York City. Brace's initiative of orphan trains eventually died out, but the idea of foster care did not. The term "foster care" was applied in that time to anyone who took in a child that was not their own, be it temporary or permanent, on their own dollar or through the financial support of an organization. What we would call today adoption was labeled then as foster care. (University of Oregon)

Brace said, "When a child of the streets stands before you in rags, with a tear-stained face, you cannot easily forget him. And yet, you are perplexed what to do. The human soul is difficult to interfere with. You hesitate how far you should go." (PBS) From before Brace's time through the early 1900s, the burden of the orphan was simply on anyone who would take up the cause. Homeless children in America could be found both in orphanages and in the homes of families; although, the trend began to change when in the early to mid 1900s more orphans were living with single families than in the 1000 orphanages found in the nation in 1910. (University of Oregon)

Foster care and adoption were two ideas distinctly divided in the New Deal of Franklin Roosevelt. The Social Security Act of 1935 offered parents in financial deprivation the opportunity to place their children elsewhere or give them up forever. Legislation was added later in the 1960s when foster care became a federally funded project. It only took ten years, but by 1970 the number of children flooding the foster care system rose to half a million. Government took the role of caring for the child under the concept of *parens patriae* which means "the duty of the state to act on behalf of the child and provide care and protection equivalent to that of a parent." (Siegle, p262) The Latin term literally means "parent of the nation".

The government has tried to be the solution to the problem to destitute souls, but the bible gives a very explicit answer to the question of this heartbreaking issue. God is the one who takes personal interest in the care of the child who goes without. "The helpless commits himself to You; You are the helper of the fatherless."(Psalm 10:14, NKJ) God has not forgotten anyone, and He certainly does not forget those who cannot help themselves. Again in Psalm 146, "The Lord watches over the strangers; He relieves the fatherless and widow" (vs. 9, NKJ). Our Lord is not in the business of exclusion. He does not want to leave out anyone, and He does not mean for us to do it either. Hosea 14:3 says that the fatherless find mercy in God. While God offers mercy, most of society at large does not offer this kind of extensive provision to anyone, especially not in reference to the underdog, where circumstances are the person's handicap. But God is different in that He specifically administers His love and mercy to those whose circumstances are their hardship.

God often calls on the heart of man to carry out the plans on *His* heart. If God intends to care for the helpless and more precisely the orphan, then these same plans are laid upon us.

Direct contrast to God's desire would be seeing these people hurt and taken advantage of. It is His purpose and focus to care for the homeless child, so anyone who comes against that purpose forcefully will have to deal with God himself. Remember in the beginning of scripture God said to Abraham "I will bless those who bless you, and I will curse him who curses you" (Genesis 12:3, NKJ). God was for Abraham, and He blessed him. So it was that anyone who came against Abraham, later understood to be all of Israel, was coming against the plans of God. The Lord did not take lightly those who came against him, saying that anyone who comes directly against God's chosen willfully is coming against Him. They would then have to deal with God's curse. So it is easy to understand that he does not make provision for and even punishes those who do the opposite of His plans. In direct statement, the Lord says there is a curse on anyone who "perverts the justice due the stranger, the fatherless, and the widow" (Deut 27:19).

Yet it seems as though the church has let this perversion into our Christian nation. Randy Bohlender said in the same sermon about prayer and adoption, "You know, it's a little crazy to me that the church has walked away from the foster care system like it has, when we are told to care for the widows and orphans. It's the only area that I can think of that the Lord has given us a mandate to do that we are happy to subcontract to the government." As though we were giving lip service to the King, but no action in faith to follow, we might find ourselves guilty of the same neglect some parents are cited for when their own children are taken away. While Christians are not the prominent figure that serves oppression to the poor, oftentimes we turn our face the other way pretending not to see the things we don't want to involve ourselves in. Perhaps we value our time, our money, or our schedule far more than we care about another person. For far too long, we have gone about our way, desiring to be uninterruptable. But true justice requires constant interruption for love's sake. The longer the church continues to ignore their call to love and act out of that love, the more evidence our corporate church gives the Lord to discontinue his blessing and consider a curse.

The bible says specifically in Zechariah not to oppress the widow or the fatherless, the alien or the poor (7:10). In fact, chapter seven is a compelling example of the sincerity of what God means when He says to follow His commands. Some men of Israel in the town of Bethel were sent with prophets "to entreat the Lord." They wanted to satisfy the Lord, and to ask honestly if they should continue fasting during the fifth month of their calendar as they had done for years and years. They were looking for an honest answer, but the answer through the prophet Zechariah came as an unexpected blow. God replied that all their fasting had amounted to nothing because they did not even do it for Him in the first place. Whoa! That might put fear in a man's heart. They had performed all this work over such a long period of time for no reward from the Lord. Something was blocking their earnest beseeching of the Lord. Do you know what was standing in the way of their good actions and pleas? God went on to say, "Administer true justice; show mercy and compassion to one another. Do not oppress the widow or the fatherless, the alien or the poor. In your hearts do not think evil of each other." (Zechariah 7:9-10, NIV 1984) God was saying 'Hey guys, you come to Me and act like you are praying and crying out. You act like you honor Me with your practices, but I tell you what: the cry of the orphan and the widow of your region is burning more loudly in my ears then what you are offering up.' God says He is not even seeing the 'great' things they are doing because of the unrighteousness they are allowing all around them.

What follows is of no less consequence. It says directly after Zechariah brings this word forth to the men, that they "refused" to listen or pay attention. In fact, it says that they stopped up their own ears - on purpose! They did not want to hear the word of the Lord. Their hearts became hard and they chose to act stubbornly. What a heart breaking reaction to the word of God! If God is speaking, He is probably speaking because He wants to give opportunity for repentance. These men, however, did not choose that route. So, it says that God became angry. Take special note that it does not say He became angry when they asked Him what to do or when they committed these terrible acts of negligence in the first place. No, his anger was aroused *after* they responded in disobedience, *after* they were given opportunity again to follow His word and then refused. God's further reaction is as follows in verses 13-14:

> 'When I called, they did not listen; so when they called, I would not listen,' says the LORD Almighty. 'I scattered them with a whirlwind among all the nations, where they were strangers. The land was left so desolate behind them that no one could come or go. This is how they made the pleasant land desolate.' (NIV 1984)

The absence of evil is not enough. We are not meant to just stand on neutral ground doing neither harm nor good. God means for us to move in positive ways because His presence is inside us. We are called to make an impact they way He would make impact. As Christians, we are ambassadors of Christ. The Lord declares in Isaiah 1:17 – "Learn to do good; Seek justice, Rebuke the oppressor; Defend the fatherless, Plead for the widow" (NKJ). We are supposed to be action-filled. The same words 'defend the fatherless' are in Psalm 82:3. The word defend in the Hebrew is *shaw-fat'*. It means "to judge; by implication to vindicate or punish; by extension to govern" (e-Sword). When Israel stood as a nation and a people in the Old Testament under God's direct rule and reign, He established ordinances and laws that would carry out righteousness. So, if a case of abuse or any other offense was committed to the orphan or widow, justice put in place by law was supposed to be carried out by the Israelites so that the helpless would be vindicated and relieved from their situation.

We see similar forms of this justice through the foundational laws of our modern society. As in the law in the Torah, the American law has both grand and detailed accounts of how to deal with the unlawful and what is to be prescribed to them. This is for the accused and the afflicted. We understand that it is against the law to murder and to steal, and each of those requires necessary legal action and consequence. A more specific topic of criminal prevention is found in child labor laws, which according to the U.S. Department of Labor, are "designed to protect the educational opportunities of youth and prohibit their employment in jobs that are detrimental to their health and safety." (Youth and Labor) The United States government has taken a stance to protect the youth within the nation, and all families and youth alike receive vindication when the law is enforced because it deters others from trying to commit the same offense. Vindication is carried out in our man-made system as we punish those who break the law. As our policy makers and law enforcers keep to the terms of all laws, they put justice into effect. Our nation's law addresses deliberate criminal action and harm in the form of negligence. As shown in the passage above, God cares as much about one as He does the other.

In addition to the heroic means of rescue from trouble, the Lord also meant for the helpless to be provided for. Even though the Hebrew culture saw the torn relationship of an orphan from his parents first, material things were still seen as a necessity. The difference from our modern day culture to theirs is the difference between material things seen as the primary loss verses a secondary loss. But of course, no father, means no income and furthermore no food. Just as much in our culture as it is in theirs, God was and is the orphan's provider, and He gave direct orders for that provision to be made manifest, not by miracles separate from the compassion of humans, or by parting the Red Sea or making food suddenly appear at the widow's table. Indeed God performs miracles all over the world on a daily basis! These are wonderful and praiseworthy for which we should give Him all the glory! However, we should not buy into the lie that we were meant to be bystanders of God's goodness, relying on Him to pull through because we decidedly would not lift a finger. He meant provision to come from Him *through* the people of Israel. He desired the hearts of those men and women to abide in His heart so that they too would have a heart of mercy.

God wanted the Israelites to so trust Him that what they gave up of their own earnings would return back to them and more by way of God's favor. This same principle applies to us today. He is asking the believer to believe what He says is right and true. He wants our hand to line up with our heart, and our heart to line up with His heart. Deuteronomy24:19 says:

> When you reap your harvest in your field, and forget a sheaf in the field, you shall not go back to get it; it shall be for the stranger, the fatherless, and the widow, that the LORD your God may bless you in all the work of your hands. (NKJ)

God knows and understands that sometimes we do our work a little sloppy. Sometimes things get dropped and sometimes left behind. In a business-driven, high-profit, goods oriented, what's-in-it-for-me world, we think efficiency and productivity are the keys to good, moral success and esteem. If nothing is wasted we praise the one who did the work. In the times of Israel, the poor lived off of what they could scrap, not from food banks and charity organizations, nor government funded programs and paper pushing institutions. The poor relied on literally what they could find, and in kind cases, the hand of their neighbor. This looks more like what we see in movies when a homeless man is digging in the dumpster and in pictures of children in South America climbing through open landfills. This is a life or death situation where a growling stomach is just about the only voice that pushes them forward. Proverbs 16:26 says, "The laborer's appetite works for him; his hunger drives him on" (NIV 1984)

God commanded a perfect economy where the poor, including the orphans and widows, would be taken care of without new institutions being built and new administration created. Farming was of course a trade that many, if not nearly all, people knew how to do and did. Instead of having the farmers dot their I's and cross their T's, He said in essence 'let the fringes go, so that my people will be satisfied.' It was instituted in the law that the poor would automatically be taken care of. And why did He say He wanted this done? Because God wanted to bless His people. He asks us to give in faith so that He can give freely to us according to His law of economy. Malachi 3:10 says, ""Bring the whole tithe into the storehouse, that there may be food in my house. Test me in this," says the LORD Almighty, "and see if I will not throw open the floodgates of heaven and pour out so much blessing that you will not have room enough to store it"" (NIV). What we see is that God has written commands in His word that will send us blessings according to the way His system works. All we have to do is what He says, and the rest is a return of love and abundance from our God.

God's word is full of these commands. He wants to thrust us into His good will. He also wants us to do it in the same heart and passion that He operates in. In Deuteronomy 24:21, God says the same thing about gathering grapes in the vineyard and leaving behind some for the poor. He describes how going over the vineyard once is the just earnings of the owner, but what is left over, where you would otherwise go back and look again for what you missed, that part is not for you. In fact, do not even go back to look the second time. What you missed is for all those who are helpless. When God talks about the grain harvest and the grapes, He is saying in essence that this practice is not just for one food or one field or one separate entity in one corner of your life. He is saying you should be offering up gifts to the poor in every area of your life, in the fields and in the vineyards.

The law did not stop with physical gifts. It goes on to describe how the people, including us, are ordered to give financial gifts. Deuteronomy 26:12-13 describes the order of how this should be done.

> When you have finished laying aside all the tithe of your increase in the third year—the year of tithing—and have given *it* to the Levite, the stranger, the fatherless, and the widow, so that they may eat within your gates and be filled, [13] then you shall say before the LORD your God: 'I have removed the holy *tithe* from *my* house, and also have given them to the Levite, the stranger, the fatherless, and the widow, according to all Your commandments which You have commanded me; I have not transgressed Your commandments, nor have I forgotten *them*.(NKJ)

Fast forward to the New Testament, and you see that Paul did not take a much different view of these original commands. He said, "Religion that God our Father accepts as pure and faultless is this: to look after orphans and widows in their distress and to keep oneself from being polluted by the world." (James 1:27, NIV) James, the brother of Jesus, was talking about what the church should be doing in pursuit of righteousness. In the New King James Version, instead of "look after", the word "visit" is used. The Greek word is *episkeptomai*, and its meaning is "to inspect, to select; by extension to go to see, relieve; look out, visit" (e-Sword). There cannot be any irony in the fact that God watches over the widow and the orphan, and the very word written here means basically to look very closely at. What God looks after, He wants us to have a heart of compassion to look after.

If someone told me to go inspect something, I am going to look in every nook and cranny I can dig my heels into, squeeze my hands through, or peer in. When you take your car to get an inspection, the mechanic does not take a long gaze at the front of your vehicle bang on the hood of the car and say "That one right there looks swell, Ms." Of course not! He would lose his job and you might get a pretty fat ticket. In reality, the mechanic gets under the hood, over the hood, behind the steering wheel, in front of the car, and behind the car. He even has to hook it up to machinery to measure things he cannot see with the human eye. That is inspection. Understand now that we are to inspect the orphan and the widow. If they live in our region, we are in charge of seeing what is going on in their world. We should see if they need clothes, food, or shelter. Do they need help finding a church or a way of transportation? Is someone mistreating them or purposefully misinforming them? You might even say we have to get nosey. I posit to say that Paul said this because the orphan is God's orphan, but it does not stop there. The orphan is our orphan. It is our duty to administer true justice through a heart of compassion and willingness to act. This is not American justice, this is godly justice. Proverbs 17:5 says, "He who mocks the poor shows contempt for their Maker, whoever gloats over disaster will not go unpunished" (NIV 1984). We should ensure we are doing what we can with what we have. In our area of responsibility, we must be sure we are found in good standing before God.

The Greek word episkeptomai can be traced to two root words epi and skopos. Epi is a superimposition relating to a number of items. We can think of it in terms of the words 'over, upon, towards, above'. The word superimpose means this: to put, lay, or stack on top of something else; to add as a dominant feature (e-Sword). Already we can see that there is a charge being given in the word. Someone else is being given some kind of upper view and hand in order for *skopos* to occur. *Skopos* means to peer about and also refers to a watch, as in a sentry or scout (e-Sword). The believer here has an inherited charge to visit, that is, to peer into the life of the orphan and widow by superimposition in order that they might be taken care of. Now, this does not mean that we go and wreak havoc by getting into personal items or situations that would embarrass, destroy, harm, or create undesirable emotions in the individual. What this word is implying is that we are to investigate and look carefully at their situation because we have compassion on them. We are to superimpose our gaze at their condition and see what is being done to them and for them with a right heart and right attitude. Where there is lack, we must take the odds and ends of our field and offer it to them. We need to direct the leftover grapes in the vineyard out of our personal pocketbook and into the hands of the needy. Proverbs 14: 31b says "whoever is kind to the needy honors God"(NIV). It is no small privilege to honor the Lord by these means.

Our motives for doing this are two-fold: first, God commanded it, and second, He is that very visitor for us. 1 John 4:19 says we love because he first loved us. We do not even have the ability to love unless we receive God's love on a personal level. The same principle applies here. God is the one who superimposes his view to look over us and check us out all the time. He comes to see how we are doing. As believers in

Christ, we are God's business, and He is the one who is over us. That love and care that is lavished over us should be the same love and care that we lavish over others.

CHAPTER

Impressing the Next Generation

There is a generation yet unknown to the world at large - infants growing in their mother's womb, children roaming the slides and swings of the neighborhood park, and teens roaming high school hallways. They are, however, known in two places: in relationship and in the statistics of social reports and tests. They are viewed as one of two things: hearts - which are either loved or thrown away, or measurable data - a tell tale of the next generation. So what is it about a generation that is so important? Why do we look at the characteristics of one generation? Why compare them to another?

To God, a day is likened to a thousand years and a thousand years a day. Because God is omnipresent and transcends time, He sees both the smallest second in one person's day and the course of an entire lifetime all in a single comprehensible moment's understanding. God sees everything from the intimate detail of a minute through our eyes to the great wars of the world fought in multiple places for many years, and He understands it all. God can see the big picture in such a way that we cannot fathom, knowing all the details, motives, and emotions of those involved. We study the big picture through facts, but God is there in the midst of them, perhaps experiencing them in multiple places as they happen. He knows the situation at large down to the very last personal detail. It is a unique view point to see something from the top looking upon it and yet from the inside looking out from it. God sees the large pieces of life in a unique way. Specifically, He sees humans, speaks to humans, and responds to humans in generations. Of course, he speaks to us individually. He sees you and me on a regular basis for what we are. He responds to our own mistakes, failures, and successes in Christ. But you and I can fathom that individual framework, simply because we relate to individuals as well, even if the depths of God's perspective in that framework are far beyond our own abilities. God sees so much more than that framework though. He sees levels and layers of time, and He relates to us as well in all other frameworks of His sight.

This God of ours is everlasting. He was never created, and He will never end. Because He is such a big God, He can see bigger chunks of time. In His greatness, He relates to a generation in addition to relating to the individual. God even labels generations. Words like 'evil', 'stubborn', and 'rebellious' describes generations in the bible who have not pleased Him. Jesus uses the words 'wicked', 'adulterous', and 'unbelieving' to describe the generation of His days here on earth. While preaching to the thousands, Peter called his generation 'corrupt' or 'perverse'. Paul called the generation he saw "warped and crooked" (Phil 2:15, NIV).

The Father also blesses and curses by generations. In Numbers 14:18 (NIV 1984), God's word says that He is not overlooking the guilty; "he punishes the children for the sin of the fathers to the third and fourth generation." Deuteronomy specifies the guilty by saying they are the ones who hate God. Similarly, the ones who love God and obey His commandments receive His kindness or blessings from the Lord for *thousands* of generations.

God makes promises to generations. He makes them to all creation, and sometimes for all creation. God spoke a promise directly to Noah, but the promise was for all generations from that moment forward. In this instance, it was also for all His creation. Every living thing received the promise that He would never again flood the earth after devastating all life that did not make it in the boat. The reminder of that promise is a rainbow. It reminds God of what He said, and it reminds us of his faithfulness and lasting word. Genesis 9:11-13 (NIV 1984) reads:

> I establish my covenant with you: Never again will all life be cut off by the waters of a flood; never again will there be a flood to destroy the earth." And God said, "This is the sign of the covenant I am making between me and you and every living creature with you, a covenant for all generations to come: I have set my rainbow in the clouds, and it will be the sign of the covenant between me and the earth."

The recipients of the promise were not only Noah and his family but "every living creature" with Noah and for "all generations to come". God was making a promise not only to Noah, but to the generation that would come after Noah and to every generation that was ever to live. This was a promise made to you and to your parents. This is a promise to your children and your great-grand children. This is a promise made to the unborn, and it is fully fulfilled now and forever. The sign was a reminder between God and "the earth". Even though giraffes and elephants are not made in the image of God, they are part of His earth's creation. They, too, receive the fullness of this promise, even if they cannot comprehend it. Beyond animals though, the earth encompasses vegetation, soil, rocks, mountains, lakes, rivers, and the list goes on. Every item that is in or on the earth receives the promise of this particular word.

Another instance of a promise addressing multiple generations is found later on in Genesis. This generational promise is different because it is not for all the earth. Abraham listened while God told him that he would be a father of many nations and kings would come from him. Again, the idea of generations is at work. God does not just want to make a promise that can only be fulfilled in a second. God wants to make promises that reach to eternity. I write that hesitantly knowing our brains cannot fathom forever. God wants promises that last as long as he does. That requires more than one lifetime. That requires many lifetimes - generations, more than we can certainly count. The Lord says to Abraham (Genesis 17:6-7, NKJ):

> "I will make you exceedingly fruitful; and I will make nations of you, and kings shall come from you. And I will establish My covenant between Me and you and your descendants after you in their generations, for an everlasting covenant, to be God to you and your descendants after you."

The sign of the covenant or promise is where we find what it is directed to and who it is for. God goes on to tell Abraham (Gen 17:10-11, NKJ):

> This is My covenant which you shall keep, between Me and you and your descendants after you: Every male child among you shall be circumcised; and you shall be circumcised in the flesh of your foreskins, and it shall be a sign of the covenant between Me and you.

This covenant or promise of God is between Himself, Abraham, and Abraham's descendants. The declaration rings true through and through, and anyone who hears of it can have understanding of it. God speaks this promise and puts it in His book so that anyone who reads it might know it. It is declared to everyone and anyone who might have ears to hear. But it is not for everyone. The promise is kept only for Abraham and his family that continues after him. The Torah says in Deuteronomy "The LORD your God will circumcise your hearts and the hearts of your descendants, so that you may love him with all your heart and with all your soul, and live." (30:6, NIV) We understand in the new covenant of Jesus Christ that the descendants of Abraham are more than just his bloodline, they are spiritual children who walk in the same faith that he pursued God with.

Our God sees in generations. It is in His very operation to see one generation from the next as unique and different from another. He mandates one generation to know Him for the first time through Abraham and another many, many years later to receive the blessing of knowing Him by inheriting the Promised Land. He mandates one generation to set foot in Egypt and another to escape it. He calls one generation to prophesy the coming of the Christ and another to live during Christ's time on earth. One generation gets to hear the Great Commission given for the first time from the lips of Jesus, while another will one day see its completion. Every generation has its time and season, its purpose as a whole. Just as each man, woman, and child has a call on their life, so the generation has a destiny to be fulfilled in it. It is always God's will that we follow Him and worship Him all the days of our life, but He calls generations to specific works and experiences unique to others. The God of all heaven and earth even says it himself (Isaiah 41:4, NIV):

> Who has done this and carried it through,
> calling forth the generations from the beginning?
> I, the LORD -with the first of them
> and with the last—I am He."

God is calling each generation forth. Only God who is all powerful and all knowing can speak to something and watch it come to fruition. He is the one who calls the generations and lets them come forth. The scripture above says He is with each one of them. The Hebrew for the word 'with' is *ayth* meaning near or among (e-Sword). This is not a distant and aloof God. But He is in the midst of our days. Here is a God that is calling, crying out, or proclaiming a generation while He is among them. There is nothing that happens without God's sovereignty. Each generation is carried by God, and He is with all of them from the beginning to the end.

While this is an awesome thing to consider, what is more considerable is that we take a look at generations through heavenly lenses, the way God sees time and people. It is a new way for us but a very old way to God. We can look to our parents and see them as individuals. If we widen our view, we can see their generation in gratitude or in reflection – learning from their ways. We can see our generation and hear the word of the Lord that is coming forth in this day to discern the times and the seasons like the sons of Issachar that we might know what we should do. We can also look at the children of the upcoming generation. As new beings in the world, they need training to know what to become. So here is where God's story intrigues – in the infancy of new life where the persistence and continuation of righteousness, holiness, mercy, love and kindness in the people of the earth hangs on the thread of a child's will and heart. Perhaps that last statement is too far gone for some to believe, but perhaps our history tells of a man who was once that hanging thread.

Noah was one man who God chose because He saw him as the last man of obedience. The bible says that "all the people on earth had corrupted their ways" (Genesis 6:12, NIV). This is not an "all" to be taken lightly. God did not make man for destruction. He did not create life for His wrath. Paul, speaking to believers, said, "For God did not appoint us to suffer wrath but to receive salvation through our Lord Jesus Christ" (1 Thessalonians 5:9, NIV). God made us for the intention of love and fellowship, but in the time of Noah, the Maker of all had lost joy in His creation and lost all hope for their return to Him. I see it almost like a depression, and yet it it's a rage. His love in abundant, vigilant care of life and His provision and wonders were all poured out for them, and yet none regarded Him. They despised God and would not look to Him. They did not care to have one glimpse of His eye. They had filled themselves, instead, with vileness that lifted a stench to God. It was such a torturous assault on the righteousness of God that in this same chapter the Lord is grieved that He even made man. Genesis 6:5-7 establishes the scene:

> The LORD saw how great the wickedness of the human race had become on the earth, and that every inclination of the thoughts of the human heart was only evil all the time. The LORD regretted that he had made human beings on the earth, and his heart was deeply troubled. So the LORD said, "I will wipe from the face of the earth the human race I have created—and with them the animals, the birds and the creatures that move along the ground—for I regret that I have made them." (NIV)

God was pulled apart, I imagine, not so much because sin was rampant or that He felt the pain of rejection, but because only one heart of multitudes was willing to be touched by His voice and be pliable to his ways. God must have sifted through one cold, hard heart after another, trying to find the few who would look to Him. Soon, the empty results had him searching for at least one. He was so pained at this point in time that He decided to literally wipe out the earth.

Forget sending down fire on Sodom and Gomorrah. This is not the exile of Judah. He is not cutting off the ten tribes of Israel. God is destroying all life on the earth, save one man and his family. God's fury was building on account of truth and justice, but his mercy was poured out for one. Noah has a beautiful testimony. Verse nine (NIV) says, "Noah was a righteous man, blameless among the people of his time, and he walked with God." His heart and will were aligned with God's. Because God found Noah to be true to Him, He decided to save the continuation of mankind through him. The continuation of godliness in man as God had created it hung on the willfulness of Noah's heart to love God.

Of course, this is a great extreme, and, of course, I do not believe God will come to destroy all mankind again on account of wickedness until the last days. On the contrary, I believe it is possible that thousands of millions of children could have the same string of love towards God as Noah had and grow up into a generation that blesses the Lord's heart. This is God's ultimate desire. That He would draw all men to Himself. What I think most Christians do not understand is that it starts with mom and dad. While we are sending evangelists into the streets, we are losing our own teenagers to selfishness and loneliness, which further turns children to alcohol, drugs, and immoral relationships. Evangelism is the mandate of God in the Great Commission, but hear this: while we gain the lost of this generation we may neglect to teach the next. We do not want to wake up in our old age to see we have lost our family in carrying the Word to the world. The Word must expand as in evangelism, but it also must continue, persisting through time, not just in space and geography. We do not have to give up one for the other, our children for our brother. We should have both.

First Lady Barbara Bush has been attributed with this quote: "Where will our country find leaders with integrity, courage, strength—all the family values—in ten, twenty, or thirty years? The answer is that you are teaching them, loving them, and raising them right now." To put it in larger context, consider America over the last one hundred years. This nation was a real beacon of light burning for Christ in so many facets because the individual was guided by Christ. But somewhere in that time, while we were out being missionaries to third world countries and winning souls on foreign soil for the last ten decades, we were slowly losing our testimony to this country, forgetting to pass down to our children what we were marching across the world for. Today, we sit in debauchery, a wasteland of pornography, captivated by alcohol and drugs, bound in chains to our personal addictions of financial gain and worshiping the god of material possession. All the while, poverty is creeping in on the 21st century market place like a small but constant leak that is soon to explode in a flood if we do not repent.

Our nation's government has gradually loosened its grip in its partnership with Israel, pushing her to give up soil to those whose ultimate purpose is to destroy her. Many wonder why we are now struggling to keep our "American" blessings. It is in great part because we have begun to curse God's chosen, and that is so because the government now in charge is part of a generation that has not received YHWY as their God, nor respected His name, not even out of moral duty.

The full onslaught of the enemy's attacks of corruption and main victories happened here in the United States in the 1960's and 70's. The hippie movement made that which is holy and had been regarded as holy since the inception of this nation into a mass common play of sin. I am talking about the sanctity of sex within the marriage covenant being torn to perversion. This was a terrible battle for Christians in this nation to loose, but a great success for hell. This one vast defeat opened the door to further degradation of human existence and worship in consecutive generations. Gangs, abortions, drugs, violence, vulgar living, lewdness, prostitution, godlessness, and the infiltration of these things in our media are only the most recent consequences in a direct sense of forgetting to tell the next generation. If we do not repent, we will further reap the judgment God has for those who refuse Him persistently, not encompassing the torture that Satan wants for us. Why, America, would you give up the blessing of God and His protection to the seemingly small and simple sin of shutting your mouth to your children? Where we have become silent, Satan has whispered, and what we have slowly begun to tolerate, has come to put a chain on us. This is how important it is to speak to the next generation. It is so crucial to the continuance of worship, that God wrote it in the book of the law. If we do not do this, we do not just loose a blessing, we gain a prison.

When the children of Israel are receiving the law for the second time in Deuteronomy right before they break out into the awesome blessing of the Promised Land, the Lord reminds them again of the first commandment. He tells the people where this first commandment should live - in their heart. And the very next verse, God says to tell these things to their children. Is it not interesting that God opted out of immediately moving on to the second commandment? Or perhaps He could have expounded on the first one. Instead God divulges on another subject completely. He tells the Israelites them how to perform the first commandment, but, peculiarly, not just in their own generation. God tells them how to love Him forever. Deuteronomy 6:4-9 (NIV) says:

> Hear, O Israel: The LORD our God, the LORD is one.
> Love the LORD your God with all your heart and

with all your soul and with all your strength. These commandments that I give you today are to be upon your hearts. Impress them on your children. Talk about them when you sit at home and when you walk along the road, when you lie down and when you get up. Tie them as symbols on your hands and bind them on your foreheads. Write them on the doorframes of your houses and on your gates.

The Lord tells us to teach the next generation. Why? Because the Lord wants a people whole heartedly for Himself. He doesn't want one generation for Himself only to see its passion die out. He wants a people to persist from generation to generation. If a mother and father are both Spanish, then naturally their child will be Spanish. God purposes that one mother in Christ and one Father in Christ will raise up a child in Christ. A natural bloodline will always persist, but a faith line must work to do so in obedience, faith, and prayer. Although, God so appreciates one heart, He desires so much more than for one man to follow Him all the days of his small vapor of a life. God is looking for a persistence to call His own. Something that will never cease to be His, some intimate lovers that will never leave His door, some wonderful remnant that will return daily just to experience the presence of their Maker. It is more than one person can fulfill. That is why God had an overwhelming resolve in His heart for the descendents of Abraham to outnumber the stars. He was so excited to have the heart of Abraham grow and flourish into a receptive and devoted nation who only wanted to love God. He wanted to see the faith of Abraham multiply a thousand ways in thousands of people, so He could relish in their presence. He just wanted to continually shine His face on those He could not stand to leave, whose hearts He ached for even before they came to life on earth.

Looking only at verse seven, the word 'impress' stands out. The meaning can be drawn by the things we understand today. Take for instance a stamp. A stamp is a molding of some symbol, picture or letter. Pressing that stamp into wax or leather produces an impression. That's what God wants us to do with the word upon our children. Moses does not tell Israel to draw a picture and show their kids. He does not say throw them in children's service and then drag them out after church. He does not say give them a million rules but never set an example for them to obey. He does not tell parents to go do ministry and forget to mention what they are living for to their kids because they are always so busy. God doesn't say parents should wear themselves out until they are too tired to pay attention to their children after getting home. He does not say to give them bibles for Christmas and birthdays and never tell them personal stories of God working in their life. None of these describe the employment of a stamp.

First, a stamp takes on the form that it is going to impress. A stamp of a flower will not impress the image of a boat. To whatever extent a mother or father follows the example and love of the Lord is the best impression that they are able give to their children. The parent has to be the cast. Jesus impresses His image on His people; He is our cast, and we are His mold. In like manner, the parents are the best concept of God the child can understand, and so the parents must be the best image of Christ separate of what they want their children to become. Second, it should be our goal to see our children succeed in spiritual matters long before earthly ones. We are to impress the importance of love before we impress the importance of grades. We are to impress the importance of prayer before we stress the importance of baseball practice. If sports or school or anything else gets in the way of the true stamp, we have to go back to scripture.

After scripture says to impress the word, subsequent verses direct us to talk about His ways all the time to our children. This is not an every once in awhile occurrence, but it is a relational activity. The difference in the scenarios above and how the word says we should teach our children about God has to do with a relationship factor. The Father wants relationships and relational experiences to be a significant factor in how we pass down our faith. The word and God's history should be an interwoven subject in the family home. We should keep his words before us and our family at all times. Verse eight says to tie the word of God as symbols on our wrists and bind them on our foreheads. The promises and decrees of God actually become reminders in the form of jewelry and other accessories. The idea is that you shouldn't be able to get away from God's word in the home the same way you can't get away from your own wrist or forehead. If anyone can get away from their own wrist and forehead, then you would be the only person to get away from God's word, and the only way to get away from the word of God at home is to literally not go home. When the children are there, they are inundated with it on the doorposts and the gates. That is how it should be in every believer's house. If our children, and all children that come into our care, are in our house, they should have the word of God blatantly before them. Moms and dads, you do not have to apologize for keeping the word before them and their grandchildren.

Proverbs 22:6 (NKJ) says to "Train a child in the way he should go, and when he is old he will not turn from it." This is explicitly God's heart. This is the prolonging of his ways through a generation to the next. It begins when the child is trained, and a child will be trained by a previous generation. After the child's training and his maturity in body and maturity in spirit, he will succeed even into old age where he is given opportunity to then train up his children and grandchildren. This is the recipe for a cycle of love forever. It was God's intentions from the beginning.

CHAPTER

9

Blessings & Curses

To the heart pains of God and the calamity of many once lovers of God, the perfect command to teach children the way of the Lord was not carried out by the first generation of Israelites who received it, and it has yet to be carried out through an entire nation to its fullest. In a prophetic song that Moses sang over Israel, he proclaimed in Deuteronomy 32:20 (NIV), "I will hide my face from them," he said, "and see what their end will be; for they are a perverse generation, children who are unfaithful."

Only three chapters before God describes the curse that would fall upon the children of later generations if they did not get rid of idols and if they continued to chase after other nations' gods. The Israelites had been tested already coming out of the 40 years of the wilderness. They received God's commands once in the past after crossing the Red Sea and entering into the desert. So now looking at this second generation, God powerfully lays down His law again to teach and warn against falling away. He reiterates the ways of holiness and righteousness and speaks of the things of the heart. Towards the end, God reveals the consequences of both faithfulness and unfaithfulness to Him and His Word. What the last generation failed at, God wants this generation to overcome, and what this generation overcomes, He wants the next to receive as their strength. It is a crucial point of trust and internal substance of the heart for God and man respectively. For God, it is the contending hope to see what this generation is made of, and for man, it is the charge to defy his wild and sinful desire and become equipped with infallible loyalty to God.

Moses first lists the blessings in chapter 28 which encompass verses 3-14, a total of 11 verses. When he introduces the subject, I can almost hear stringed instruments in the background building the momentum of a highly anticipated and yet sober moment. He says, "If you fully obey the LORD your God and carefully follow all His commands I give you today, the LORD your God will set you high above all the nations on earth. All these blessings will come on you and accompany you if you obey the LORD your God." He is speaking of God's provision, His everlasting hand and never-ending goodness. Just as a replica of God's throne on earth was portrayed in the tabernacle, a replica of a heaven-like atmosphere was to be ever with these people. God's kindness was to endure with Israel as long as their hearts' willingness could stand. The first listed blessings read (Deut 28:3-6, NIV):

> You will be blessed in the city and blessed in the country.
> The fruit of your womb will be blessed, and the crops of your land and the young of your livestock—the calves of your herds and the lambs of your flocks.
> Your basket and your kneading trough will be blessed.
> You will be blessed when you come in and blessed when you go out.

I like these verses very much because, first, they are powerful, even to speak over your own life, but second, they reach every main part of community life. In my own paraphrase God would say, 'Hey you guys in down town! You guys are going to be at peace and will have my love. You guys out in the sticks, you guys will have it good, too. And you know what, I'm not going to give it to just you, your kids are going to have what you have. By the way, the gross income of your businesses will have gain. I mean to tell you, you're going to be so blessed; your fruit will have fruit! Who else is gonna do that for ya? Huh? Come on. And there will be so much food; you will need to exercise to work it off. When you take your business out, you're going to get blessed, and when you're traveling back home, I'm giving you all the protection and support you need.'

The Lord only goes on in the next paragraph with more lavish words. He pours it on like honey and does not apologize. Among them, is the promise that their enemies will be defeated, and they won't be barely defeated. The enemies are going to be so scared out of their minds that they won't even stick together and go the way they came. They will be sent fleeing seven ways. The scriptures develop further to say that all people on earth will fear the Israelites. Beyond that, God is going to "open the heavens, the storehouses of His bounty." These guys are going to be rich! Not filthy rich, holy rich!

Next, chapter twenty-eight moves on to the curses. These start in verse 16 and finish in verse 68, totaling 52 verses of cursing. (Not that kind of cursing. Think holy cursing.) I am a numbers person; so let's do numbers. If we were to calculate percentages, sixteen percent of chapter twenty-eight are blessings, and over seventy-five percent are cursings. Why does God want to talk about the bad more than the good? I think one reason is evident: deterrence. If you can remember what will happen by going the wrong way, then you have a pretty good shot of deciding against that action which lends to the severe punishments listed.

Every believer should read these. No exceptions. If the Israelites had to stand there outside in the beating sun under the command of Moses for hours while they endured those words, you should, too. However, I know no one really wants to read them for pleasure. If you have never read the curses, today's your day. This section of scripture is absolutely frightening in content. I don't mean to say that it is hard to hear 52 ongoing verses describing the possibility of a harsh future. I mean that with each verse the curses get increasingly more and more disastrous. It's exponential. (Told you I'm a numbers person.) The intensity escalates until it is nearly obscene. I encourage you to read them, though. In fact, read the whole chapter. That will bring you to a depth these words cannot. To outline the first few curses which are of mild tone compared to the later, let us look at Deuteronomy 28:16-19 (NIV):

> You will be cursed in the city and cursed in the country.
> Your basket and your kneading trough will be cursed.
> The fruit of your womb will be cursed, and the crops of your land, and the calves of your herds and the lambs of your flocks.
> You will be cursed when you come in and cursed when you go out.

These verses are the kind that makes your spirit sink, and this is not even the horrendous part of the chapter. Listen to my laymen's interpretation. 'You cannot escape your hopelessness no matter where you go. You will never have enough food, and when you think you do, it will be rotten. If in your pain and suffering, your only hope is that your children will have it different than you do, think again. They will not be able to break away from the situation you have inherited. Your financial gain will come to ruin, and your plans, business endeavors, and work will fail. You will be rejected when you leave your home, and spat on when you walk back in.'

Can these conditions be any more polar opposite? The first says you cannot flee from your blessing, no matter where you end up. The curse says you cannot leave your misery no matter how hard you kick. Regardless of how desperate you come searching, opportunity will not arise. Can I just tell you this is hard for me to write? I am having to stop and breathe and take in what we are reflecting on. Even though I have already read the curses many times over in different seasons of my life, explaining them makes my heart drop. Expanding on this feels like expanding on hell. This is like real hopelessness . . . Even if a people turn and repent and if God relents, the season of cursing is like nothing I want to know.

There is so much I could walk us through, but I feel like there are two verses the Lord wants to highlight. Contemplate them as you read the scriptures. The first is verse 22 (NIV), "The LORD will strike you with wasting disease, with fever and inflammation, with scorching heat and drought, with blight and mildew, which will plague you until you perish." The second is verse 28 (NIV), "The LORD will afflict you with madness, blindness and confusion of mind." Though there may be words to say how these have crept into society, you can see them much clearer and understand them better when you turn on the evening news. I will let your favorite news anchor describe the effects of such terrible consequence.

The next chapter describes how the cursed land will look from other nations' perspectives. The curse does not end with direct afflictions, but the agony wears on in a failing name and a despised reputation. Deuteronomy 29: 22-24 (NIV) says,

> "Your children who follow you in later generations and foreigners who come from distant lands will see the calamities that have fallen on the land and the diseases with which the LORD has afflicted it. The whole land will be a burning waste of salt and sulfur— nothing planted, nothing sprouting, no vegetation growing on it. It will be like the destruction of Sodom and Gomorrah, Admah and Zeboyim, which the LORD overthrew in fierce anger. All the nations will ask: "Why has the LORD done this to this land? Why this fierce, burning anger?"

Attention will be drawn to the desolate land from "all nations", and the people of this nation will not be able to hide from their shame. It trails them not just in one lifetime but for many. The Lord has an answer to this dire 'why' that everyone cries out.

"The answer will be: "It is because this people abandoned the covenant of the LORD, the God of their fathers" (Deut 29:25, NIV 1984). It is already easy enough to leave the faith in the world we live in. Let us not make it any easier for our children by never teaching them the faith in the first place. How awful is it to say that the God of the fathers is not the God of the sons? It tears at my center with heart-wrenching twists. The punishment the later generations of Israel received is that God hid His face from them. Believe me, we do not want God to hide His face from us. What a terrible thing for any people to be left alone to the atrocities of sin and hopelessness. The stark contrast to this scenario is His full blessing. In numbers, Moses recites the Levitical priestly blessing Aaron is to give to the Israelites. "The LORD bless you and keep you; the LORD make His face shine on you and be gracious to you; the LORD turn His face toward you and give you peace." (6:24-26) Not only does the blessing include God turning His face toward us, it talks about a shining from His face on the people. To understand correctly if we want a great blessing from the Lord, we want His face. Let us learn from this history that it is incumbent upon us to be the stamp and to make the impression of godliness, so that the next generation has a predominating chance to love the Lord our God.

Our nation's beloved president who rose to the occasion of moral character and godly resolve led us through the bloodiest war America has known that we might come out to serve God on the other side. Although his life was full of suffering, he conquered much. In 1818, his family was forced out of their home, and he was forced to work to provide for them. Over the next 18 years his mother died, and his business failed. He lost his job, and he went bankrupt. His fiancé died before he married her. He had a nervous breakdown, was bedridden, and didn't recover for six months. He ran for a variety of political offices and lost eight times during the course of his political trials.

Through his perseverance great character was laid in him. The foundational mentorship he had with John Quincy Adams gave him brilliant understanding of the power in generational baton passes. "A child is a person who is going to carry on what you started. He's going to sit where you are sitting and when you are gone, attend to the things which you think are important...The fate of humanity is in his hand," said Lincoln. Lincoln carried on the vision for the ending of slavery that John Q. Adams so adamantly worked for in his generation. Because of the passion and determination Lincoln received from his guide, counselor, and for lack of a better word, his father figure, he was able to continue the fight and win. God effactually put Lincoln in charge of the ending of our nation's great sin. For better or for worse, every father and every generation instills something in the next.

For every generation of Israel's history, another had gone before and taught her the ways they practiced. In Judges 2:10 (NIV, 1984) it says, "After that whole generation had been gathered to their fathers, another generation grew up, who knew neither the LORD nor what He had done for Israel." This is such a sorrowful scripture, like great expectancy of what the former had done plundered by the fruit in the next, but we can learn vast wisdom from it. The generation that grew up in the Promised Land did not know the Lord. That speaks one of two possibilities. The first is that the parents introduced the Lord to the younger generation, but the children rejected God and all that He had done. It is devastating if an entire generation rejected truth, especially if they are being taught and shown all God did. A second possibility suggests the parents never introduced the Lord to their kids. This second scenario finds the parents guilty. In that case, the younger generation may not have known what the Lord had done for Israel. The parents may not have told the stories of the Red Sea and the frightened faces of the Egyptians. They may not have read the book of the Law or taught the faithfulness of God. This is the more likely scenario because the children, the scripture says, did not know what God had done for them, meaning no one had told them. Here is where the buck stops. The parents did not impress the history and the commandments on their children.

I feel a sort of despondency and sullen regard for the ending fortunes of both generations in Israel: the one who entered the Promised Land and the children of that generation. The first generation may have missed a grandiose opportunity to preserve what God had given them in the forthcoming generation. The next generation could have chosen to know God and follow all His ways. They could have had it all, in terms of blessings, had they been told what God said. But the word says that they did not know God. We will not know in this lifetime if that was their outright decision in blatant rebellion of what was taught them or if it was never passed on. One thing holds true: God made a way for His people to follow Him beyond one lifetime, and His people did not take it.

Just paragraphs after scripture speaks of impressing the word on our children, the Lord says, (Deuteronomy 6:20-25, NIV 1984):

> In the future, when your son asks you, "What is the meaning of the stipulations, decrees and laws the LORD our God has commanded you?" tell him: "We were slaves of Pharaoh in Egypt, but the LORD brought us out of Egypt with a mighty hand. Before our eyes

the LORD sent miraculous signs and wonders—great and terrible—upon Egypt and Pharaoh and his whole household. But He brought us out from there to bring us in and give us the land that He promised on oath to our forefathers. The LORD commanded us to obey all these decrees and to fear the LORD our God, so that we might always prosper and be kept alive, as is the case today. And if we are careful to obey all this law before the LORD our God, as He has commanded us, that will be our righteousness."

God made it so easy; He even wrote the very words down that parents should respond to their child with. I hear many parents wish aloud that their children came with a manual. Well, look what we found! The only thing the Israelites of that generation had to have done was to open the book and read it verbatim. God says "tell him", meaning tell the child these words. He even made it quotable! You cannot get any easier than this. God mandated the Israelites to tell about the personal experiences and miracles of their generation and the one before them. In the same way, we should share with our children our personal experiences with God and testimonies of how he brought us into the kingdom. Parents should appropriately layer their transparency so that, at the right ages, children can know even where their parent's failings were and how the Lord's faithfulness pulled them out of the pit. Story after story can be shared to effectually build our children's faith. Of course, every Christian must continually read the bible with devotion and seek to understand truth. In addition, I believe that just as believers are to build each other up with personal testimonies and prayer, we should also be building up our children. We can offer them a tangible reality of stories from people they know and see. It will bring a different dimension to the entire understanding of anyone's faith, and I believe this was God's intention among generations. A child has no foundation of God when he or she is born and usually nothing in their known world to base their faith on. Parents can provide a starting point, a spring board so to speak, from which to help unleash the child's inner faith and begin building their own personal walk. When a child hears a testimony, his spirit has the opportunity to grasp it in faith and believe what God has done in the other person's life.

The book of Job talks about seeking the older generation. If our children could cry out in understanding they might say this: "Ask the former generations and find out what their fathers learned, for we were born only yesterday and know nothing, and our days on earth are but a shadow" (8:8-9, NIV 1984). Psalm 78:4b (NIV 1984) is the epitome of what every parent should proactively say to their child. "We will tell the next generation the praiseworthy deeds of the LORD, His power, and the wonders He has done." What stories can you pass down? So many adults that get saved later in life so often say things like 'I never knew.' and 'If only I had been told.' Verse 6 (NIV 1984) explains why we should not hide the things the Lord has done. It says "so the next generation would know them, even the children yet to be born, and they in turn would tell their children." Making the teachings of Christianity impersonal is totally out of character with Christianity itself. Christianity is very personal and very intimate, but it doesn't need to be private. Unveiling your secret experiences with God at the expense of exposing past sins and failures is no expense at all. That lie is from hell, and it comes because telling your story is such a powerful one. Our generation has the potential to rise up and do such a magnificent work in passing down the faith.

The same theme is found in Psalm 145:4 (NIV 1984), "One generation will commend your works to another; they will tell of your mighty acts." God is not pretentious in giving us His commands. He has set up the world and the universe so that his commands are what fulfills all for establishing his kingdom. There is no other way to go about it. To be kingdom minded means to be generationally minded. If God is to persist in the hearts and minds of mankind we must tell the ones who will inhabit the earth after us. Otherwise, what good are our works if the full purposes of those works are not accomplished in our life? But, if faith can be regenerated in a new people, then perhaps the full purpose will be worked out in their life. Consider the author of the book of Joel when he talks about the repercussions of sin affecting a multitude in Israel. He is crying out for his people to turn and repent. He wants them to remember what their dire physical circumstances have come to as a result of leaving the one true God. "Tell it to your children, and let your children tell it to their children, and their children to the next generation."

But I believe God has a prescription for those who do not leave him. Psalm 24 describes a people that are entirely different than the norm this world sees. It is a picture of a select chosen or an uncommon jewel. It seems to insinuate a rarity among men. Verse 3 (NIV) says, "Who may ascend the hill of the Lord? Who may stand in his holy place?" The question is stated as almost futile, as if it were an impossibility. It comes at almost a mocking tone, like it was daring someone to be so presumptuous to say he could stand in that place. The answer comes in verse 4. "The one who has clean hands and a pure heart, who does not trust in an idol or swear by a false god." This is a hard verse, too.

The bible says that all have sinned and fallen short. No one is perfectly pristine. Well, not all by themselves. And then, who has a pure heart? Doesn't God know our inner most thoughts? In the Gospels, didn't Jesus always seem to know other men's thoughts or what was in their hearts? I don't think any corrupt or sinful thought can escape God. But still these are the requirements for going to God. This person should not trust in an idol. That means he cannot worship an idol or pray to one. That means money cannot be trusted more than God. Jobs and the economy cannot be this man's first look for resolve. This person cannot swear by what is false. They cannot be double minded, but they also cannot speak lies out of the side of their mouth. They cannot profess something wrong in order to save themselves or their reputation.

With all these requirements, it seems like it is quite an impossibility. Or if it is possible, it appears that not many would attain it. However, verse five goes on to describe the reward of such who can follow through. "They will receive blessing from the Lord and vindication from God their Savior." If someone can possibly attain all the conditions in order to have the grace to approach God, then God is going to bless them. This is not just butter on the bread, this is His hand of protection and His elevation to new heights. This is His boldness for his work and riches for the house. God's blessings are great, however He may chose to impart them. God will also defend that person against their enemies. God is going to be this person's general and army.

He is the direct protection for him. In other words, there is no reason to fear because God is on your side.

What a beautiful description for this thing we would all love to obtain! But wait – God has one more thing to say about it. Verse 6 (NIV) says, "Such is the generation of those who seek him, who seek your face, God of Jacob." A generation? The writer, and God too, is implying that a generation can have this. It was just in verse 4 where we questioned if it was even a feasible thing for a human to accomplish, but now God is saying it is a generation that can have this. What if an entire generation of believers could receive blessings and vindication from the Lord? That would be remarkable thing the world would marvel at. God is saying it is more than possible. He is waiting for an entire generation to arise and do this thing! But what generation will it be?

If we rewrote verses 3-5 with this new understanding, with the answer to the question in mind, it would look something like this:

> Who may ascend the mountain of the Lord? The generation of those who seek Him.
> Who may stand in His holy place? Those who seek your face, God of Jacob.
> The generation who seeks God has clean hands and pure heart. Those who seek His face do not trust in an idol or swear by what is false.
> The generation who seeks Him will receive the blessing from the Lord. Those who seek your face, God of Jacob, will receive vindication from God their Savior.

Suddenly, it is an easy thing. It is an intimate thing. Those who would seek God and His face are the ones with an undivided heart who are loyal to God and His ways. They are the ones that are continually before God searching Him out. And if we would be continually before God, always talking about Him and studying Him, what time would we have to worship other gods? What would compel us to lie? Nothing, as long as we stay steadily before Him. Then we may go up to the holy place as He gives us clean hands and a pure heart by the blood of Jesus Christ. He did not limit this to one person, His select few, or designate it an unachievable task. God says He will pour out His blessing on the generation who will do it. We have the power to begin the stirring of this vision by teaching the next generation relentlessly and loving them passionately. This could be the generation the psalmist spoke of. The blessing that could then follow would fall on our nation and our bloodlines.

Our Generation 10

Our generation is the generation we see before our very eyes - all those living right now. Specifically, the young and upcoming generation has been labeled the fatherless generation, an ill-phrase of resounding destruction that pains me even to write it, but in so many ways it is true to its name. We have seen fathers abandon all the responsibility of their household, the place where they should take pride in building a heritage to their life. Instead the devil has distorted their thinking to see children not as a blessing but as the exact opposite of what God's word declares, an utter lie from the prince of lies. Children are carried, accepted, and treated as regrettable burdens. No longer are fathers fighting for the child. More and more often they flee the responsibility being enveloped in their own cloud of selfishness in order to preserve their life. Albeit while in search of their own life's preservation, they only lose it. Sadly, this is not a plague contracted only by men, but women also. Mothers and fathers are walking out the door of their children's lives never to return again. Some are searching for numbing medicines to annihilate life's pains through alcohol and drugs, all the while their escapism whisks them away from the role they are meant to assume in the helpless lives of the next generation beneath them. Others subtly decide to slip into the art of casting off this responsibility by maintaining physical presence in the home like a ghost having no affect or interaction with the family members. Different from absenteeism, laziness may creep in through the degraded habits of friends and relatives, most often the parents' parents. The bible says "If anyone does not provide for his relatives, and especially for his immediate family, he has denied the faith and is worse than an unbeliever" (1 Tim 5:8, NIV 1984). A parent who doesn't work could mean five people who don't eat.

But the sickness does not end with mere absentee-ism. Divorce rates are now being reported at over 50%. The church has now preceded her reputation by beating the nation's average with her own embarrassing statistic, hovering a few percentage points over it. Children are left behind while parents serve time behind prison bars. Poverty is a large concern for our society especially when it comes to single moms. Children under the age of 18 (25% of the U.S. population) account for 40% of all Americans living in poverty. The reason for this is single moms single-handedly "are the fastest growing segment of the overall poverty population."(Kendall, p 39) Even more devastating, families with children encompassed 40% of the entire U.S. homeless population in 2004 (Kendall, p 41). Two other factors that highly effect the upcoming generation are abortion and foster care.

The National Right to Life Educational Trust Fund wrote an article in January of 2010 estimating 52,008,665 abortions had been preformed since the 1973 Roe v. Wade court decision. (National Rights to Life) Other Christian sources are reporting an estimated 57 million current in 2014. We have fast exceeded the 50 million mark of aborted lives that we have heard preached about over the last few years. These deaths have left an empty hole in society. Most people haven't noticed. However, economists have researched and shown what could have been at play today in the housing industry. For instance, if some of those 50 million were alive in adulthood and purchasing homes as the average American does around age 40, the outcome would not have been so bleak for the real estate market. Although social security is not the answer to our life's most critical needs, as some would argue, lives of working citizens numbering somewhere in the 12-15 million range (constituting those who would be alive today if not aborted) would have nearly satisfied the current situation in social security today. That working class, now absent from our U.S. population, would be paying a large amount into the system. It would not be a permanent fix, but it might have bought some time for such a necessary and emergent need of systematic repair, slowing down social security's race to the red and allowing time to discuss the most beneficial and reasonable solutions. The baby boomer generation was the generation that began legal abortion. Perhaps their generation would not be as comparatively large to their children's generation if they hadn't aborted about 1 million babies per year.

One online blogger, Justin Taylor from The Gospel Coalition website, illustrated how many lives were crying out in this way. He cited combined populations of Kentucky, Oregon, Oklahoma, Connecticut, Iowa, Mississippi, Arkansas, Kansas, Utah, Nevada, New Mexico, West Virginia, Nebraska, Idaho, Maine and 10 more states to demonstrate a present day equivalent of the people murdered in this nation through abortion alone (Taylor). To put it plainly, that would be like destroying one sixth of our living U.S. population. The only problem is that it is not a 'like'; it is actually the number of people that have been killed. They are all in reality dead. If tomorrow the populations of all 25 states that Justin Taylor named were altogether taken out by acts of war, it would represent the closest reality check to the profound devastation our nation has suffered in population loss to abortion. The only difference, I fear, would be like in the case of the September 11th attack, America would mourn greatly over the act of war and even memorialize it where she never shed a tear for her own lost children.

Abortion stands today as "one of the most common surgical procedures for women of reproductive age" (Ortiz-Portillo 48). A study done in New Orleans, Louisiana in 2006 surveyed a population of women who entered an abortion clinic. This sample geared its research, among the other dimensions of pregnancy, toward the reasons for seeking an abortion. The three most common reasons for seeking an abortion were "cannot afford a child", "not ready for a child", and "does not want anymore children". The next two most common reasons following were that they were not married or they were in a relationship with an unstable man (Santelli 2012). Consider the fact that 48.2%, nearly half, of the abortion clinic sample decided upon abortion because they could not afford the child (Santelli 2012).

Dr. Bernard Nathanson, one of the founders of the NARAL organization of 1969 standing for National Association for the Appeal of Abortion Laws, put it this way in his documentary, entitled The Silent Scream, "The destruction of a living human being is no solution to what is basically a social problem." When a mother (and father) chooses to kill their child in order to solve a social dilemma, then the consented death of human life only places larger implications of social, national, and spiritual issues at stake.

Besides social security, the housing industry, and a list of other affected regions due to the missing fifty million, the word of God speaks boldly about the matter. The story of Cain and Abel illustrates the first recorded incident of murder. Both men go to make offerings to the Lord, but only Abel's gift was received with favor. Cain is of course upset and deeply disturbed. Instead of going to God for reconciliation, he turns his pain into anger and lets jealousy take root. Sin takes its full course and produces death, this time not only in the spiritual life of the one sinning but in the physical life of his brother Abel. Now the Lord gives us some insight into the situation in Genesis 4:10. "The LORD said, "What have you done? Listen! Your brother's blood cries out to me from the ground"" (NIV). We know that God knows all things at all times, so no one has to tell him that Abel was murdered. God simply knew, but He also heard a cry – from the blood of Abel. It seems possible that the spilled blood of the murdered or innocent blood sends up a cry to God and not just any cry.

This is a cry that we know two things about: first, God hears it. Take note of that because God does not listen to all cries that are sent up to Him. While God is talking to the persistently rebellious Israel, He says, "When you spread out your hands in prayer, I hide my eyes from you; even when you offer many prayers, I am not listening. Your hands are full of blood!" (Isaiah 1:15, NIV) We know from both the Old New Testament, that

God does not hear the unrighteous. Second, God tells Cain to "listen" for the cry that He has already heard. That means that Cain had the potential to hear the same cry that God heard coming from the blood of Abel. I believe this is a spiritual cry heard by the human spirit.

We might ask why does the cry come from the blood? Leviticus 17:11a says, "For the life of the flesh is in the blood" (NKJ). This is the very life inside the body which God made to be the sustaining contributor of that body. We understand this principle in today's secular society. If someone is badly wounded and loosing blood, the bleeding must be stopped or the person could die. A wound might not be fatal, but, if left unattended over a certain period of time, the injured person might slowly drift in and out of consciousness until their life leaves them. Most citizens will give blood to donation banks in order for those who need blood to recover from any number of ailments or for those who need a vital blood transfusion. Giving blood often saves lives. Blood is a basic essential of life. Now if God calls it the life of the flesh, then we should assume there is power in it. This should sound familiar. The blood of Jesus comes to mind.

He died one time for all people in all decades and centuries to live under the protection of his blood. How can this be? Because while the enemy stands for death, God said there is life in his blood. When Jesus died on the cross for all humanity to have eternal life, His blood ran down on Calvary's cross. His blood produces life.

Imagine that an unborn child murdered in the mother's womb, whose blood cries out to heaven by default, is heard by the Lord of Hosts. This is a powerful ringing in the ears of the Almighty. We know that Cain suffered some heavy consequences for what he did when he murdered a righteous man. But what about murdering one before life was offered to him, when God was the entity who planned and decidedly set that life in motion? If the fear of the Lord has not come upon you yet, let's multiply the single instance by fifty million and extend the time from one hour to over forty years (the time of the instituted amendment from Roe v. Wade until now). The equivalent to one sixth of the current U.S. population has blood that is and has been crying out to the Lord of Hosts for over half a generation. The Lords wrath is stirring because the innocent are crying out, and heaven is hearing. Listen! Our childrens' blood cries out to God from American soil, and we should be able to hear their cry, too. Let it ring in ears of your spirit that we might stand up and be moved to repentance and administer true justice.

The law given in the Torah addresses murder or "bloodshed", as it is called. Numbers 35:33-34 (NIV) so poignantly declares,

> "'Do not pollute the land where you are. Bloodshed pollutes the land, and atonement cannot be made for the land on which blood has been shed, except by the blood of the one who shed it. Do not defile the land where you live and where I dwell, for I, the LORD, dwell among the Israelites.'"

I would like to suppose that as Christians we long to have God dwell among us. We long to feel Him, hear Him, and get close to Him. We want His presence and peace greatly not only in our secret place but also across this nation. We desire His presence and favor with our people. But here is a hard word, a word of conviction for what we have done and what we continue to do. God said that bloodshed pollutes the land. Besides the murders that happen every day which are regarded as crime by our country's current law, we are sending up an additional million every year by abortion, and our law does not account it as criminal. America has positioned herself to decidedly stand against the justice of God, and so this makes her guilty of the sin. Our land is extravagantly inundated with pollution. Every nook and cranny is mixed with the blood of lives that were not ours to take. There is only one ramification for the shedding of blood, and it is the blood of the one who shed it. Again Genesis says, "Whoever sheds human blood, by humans shall their blood be shed; for in the image of God has God made mankind" (9:6, NIV). In other words, the Lord is coming for the life of the one who took life. But Jesus, who bore our sins on a cross, took away the sin of the world. This produces an option. The author of Hebrews writes, "You have come to God, the Judge of all . . . to Jesus the mediator of a new covenant, and to the sprinkled blood that speaks a better word than the blood of Abel" (Hebrews 12:23b-24, NIV). Jesus' blood has a testimony that outweighs the testimony of unrighteousness – even murder. Not only does it cover our sin, but it washes it clean away. We can repent and be clothed by the most powerful life in existence – Jesus' blood, or we can stand against God, choose not to receive His mercy, and receive the full onslaught of the consequences and repercussions of our sins just like the stiff-necked generation of Israel. If the later is our choice, blood is still required for the bloodshed. Atonement will be made for one way or the other. The decision is laid before us.

The consequences of a non-repentive heart are devastating. Listen to the Lord speak to the Israelites in Ezekiel 9:9-10 (NIV 1984):

> He answered me, "The sin of the house of Israel and Judah is exceedingly great; the land is full of bloodshed and the city is full of injustice. They say, 'The LORD has forsaken the land; the LORD does not see.' So I will not look on them with pity or spare them, but I will bring down on their own heads what they have done."

What the Israelites said about God, so many in our nation are saying about Him today. They said 'The Lord does not see', and our nation moves in like fashion kicking against God. The self-righteous say he does not know anything. Others claim there is a benevolent and aloof god, who either doesn't understand or doesn't care what we are doing, as if the human race can administer their own unjust laws and evade retribution. Numbers of Americans say He does not even exist. The city of a hardened heart receives the consequence of verse ten. God said that He would not spare them. I do not want to imagine what God would do to our nation if He brought down on our own heads what we have done. Remember those 25 states discussed earlier? I cannot imagine what horror that would look like, and quite frankly, I sincerely hope we do not have to find out. My beckoning call is that we chose the blood of Jesus, and start walking the other way.

Some might say that those particular consequences were made only for the Israelites because they were descendents of God's chosen people. They were to be His chosen forever. I will introduce to you the prophecy to Edom, a non-chosen, non-God fearing people. It comes from the same book of Ezekiel, this time found in chapter 35, verse 6. "Therefore as surely as I live, declares the Sovereign LORD, I will give you over to bloodshed and it will pursue you. Since you did not hate bloodshed, bloodshed will pursue you" (NIV 1984) God's law is God's law. It applies to all people everywhere. There are no excuses because His law is written on our hearts, and nature reveals His majesty. "For since the creation of the world God's invisible qualities— his eternal power and divine nature—have been clearly seen, being understood from what has been made, so that people are without excuse."(Romans 1:20, NIV) We cannot point fingers. We cannot slough off the blame. Nobody made us do it. The consequences are the same for us all, unless our community wholly chooses the blood of Jesus for our atonement.

It is a woe to those who are not under the blood. Proverbs 1:11(NIV) describe those who destroy lives saying they "lie in wait for innocent blood" and "ambush some harmless soul". Proverbs says how they do this for their own personal gain. We can peer into the scene of the ungodly as they engage in perverted conversation in verses 13-14. "We will get all sorts of valuable things and fill our houses with plunder; throw in your lot with us, and we will share a common purse" (NIV1984). It might not look the same since our impregnated are not necessarily killing for gold or silver, but convenience is a personal gain sought after in and of itself. I dare say the faculties providing abortion services may well be sharing a common purse amongst themselves in the industry. Gain is gain. But verse 18 says, "These men lie in wait for their own blood; they waylay only themselves!" (NIV 1984). Interesting how God's law works that when men seek to kill, they end up losing their own life.

Israel among so many other sins, committed one which was detestable to the Lord. They offered their children and babies up to idol worship, to a god in the bible called Molech, the god of the Ammonites. This god was worshipped by offering children's lives to him. The worshippers would literally throw their children into a fire where they would burn alive. They thought they were winning clout with another nation's god, and it was a detestable thing to the Lord. King Josiah, who took his rule at age eight, came onto the scene during Israel's prostitution to other gods. Under Josiah's rule the book of the law was found while the temple was being cleaned out, and Josiah was immediately convicted at the heart when he found that Israel should not be worshiping any other god. 2 Kings 23:10 states, "[King Josiah] desecrated Topheth, which was in the Valley of Ben Hinnom, so no one could use it to sacrifice his son or daughter in the fire to Molech" (NIV 1984). Here is a sign of hope that we, too, can tear down the strongholds which keep our country from worshiping the wrong gods and stop the bloodshed of the innocent. We should pray for our leaders to become like King Josiahs. They must find God, His Word, and have personal revelation in their hearts to lead them and our nation to this kind of Holy Spirit led action.

God said in Jeremiah 19, "For they have forsaken me and made this a place of foreign gods . . . and they have filled this place with the blood of the innocent. They have built the high places of Baal to burn their children in the fire as offerings to Baal—something I did not command or mention, nor did it enter my mind" (vs. 4-5, NIV). The practice of killing innocent life, especially of babies never entered God's mind until He saw it. Abortion, this infanticide, to Him, was beyond wicked. It is a kind of self-hatred. Killing the next generation is killing your own kind. What makes it any different if our parents did it to us? If I could put it in different words, God said it was unthinkable. He knew we were capable of evil once Adam and Eve fell, but this is intolerable. It is almost as if He says to us, 'This is pure, devoted self-destruction – I don't even understand how you brought yourselves to think it up.' Yet we walk around in the 21st century like it's no more unnatural than getting a bite to eat.

As it stands yet, we are looking infanticide in the face. We are committing genocide by the millions, cleansing our nation of the unborn. We are killing a generation that had yet to produce themselves. We are not any different from the Israelites who threw their children to death in the raging fire. Americans are throwing away the lives of their children and grandchildren only to exalt the god of self, in the name of convenience and ego-cultural values. Because we stand for ourselves and for no one else, we are producing a culture that moves for no one. Oh, how we are polluting our land with this atrocity!

The definition for the word abortion has some shocking value. Of course the word abortion is used as a general term in figurative language as well as today's common place use - a forced terminated pregnancy. The second definition stands as one word: monstrosity. It has become quite a monster indeed. Further research shows the word monstrosity defined by Webster as something "deviating from the norm". Abortion is a deviation from what is supposed to be normal under the laws of nature and God's law. It is defined as "an object of great and often frightening size, force, or complexity". The definition goes on to say it is "an excessively bad or shocking example." This sounds too convicting to be true, but I do not believe it is mere coincidence. How can our nation deem zero value in the life of a human, made in the image of God and whose soul's value is limitless? We kill the very item which has no price, and yet we are demanded to pay for the thing which can never be paid for . . . except under the blood of Jesus.

If you are considering abortion, consider adoption. Some other lover of Jesus wants desperately to love the child of your womb. They so desire to give a child everything he or she needs in life with love. See it as a righteous and holy thing. Choosing life is considering the life inside you as precious, and it honors God. God says to the believer that He has "set before you life and death, blessing and cursing; therefore choose life, that both you and your descendants may live; that you may love the LORD your God, that you may obey His voice, and that you may cling to Him, for He is your life and the length of your days" (Deut 30:19b-20, NKJ). You can have the blessing of the Lord and be covered in His protection. He will be your life and grant you peace. To others who are not considering abortion but know of women or couples who are, speak life to these people. Encourage them in the Lord to save the life within them. Even if it is not decidedly theirs to raise, it will be someone else's joy, and the Lord will be honored by them and bless them for loving life. For those who have already experienced abortion, there is hope. You can turn to the Lord with your heart this very minute and ask for forgiveness. As you submit your past, present and future to Him, He will cover you with his goodness and mercy. It only takes a repentant heart to receive Jesus' blood that washes it all away. Your child is in heaven, and if you accept Jesus as King of your life, you will one day have the joy of meeting your child and being united with his or her heart.

While abortion is such a heavily publicized topic and constantly demands attention from believers and nonbelievers, another topic remains largely hidden. American foster care is the nation's largest babysitter and guardian to infants and youth alike. Foster care is most commonly understood today as the holding grounds for children whose parents have abandoned or abused them, and all in all, that is correct. What most people do not know is how many children enter the system, and what happens to them once they are in.

The total number of children served in American foster care over the course of any given year ranges from 700,000 to 800,000 children. From the 1990's to the 2000's, U.S. foster care has hovered over a half million in population. For the first time in a long time, that number dropped below the half million mark in September of 2007 at 489,000 children. The number has continued to drop in small increments.

A report written in 2008 by Dr. William P. O'Hare under Kids Count project of the Annie E. Casey Foundation entitled "Data on Children in Foster Care from the Census Bureau" found that the living situations of most foster care children were less advantageous compared to the children of the general population in the U.S. The finding showed that households with foster care children typically have a larger ratio of children to adults, are less likely to be married-couple households, and are more likely to be single-parent or cohabitating-couple households. Other measures showed households with foster care children are more likely to be in low-income families (income less than 200 percent of the poverty line), have a lower average household income, are more likely to have a severe financial housing burden (contributing more than 30 percent of income to housing), and are more likely to report receiving public assistance income.

The foster care system was established to take children out from difficult situations and help place them somewhere they can thrive and remain in safety. As the outcome shows, the place they are sent to, even in a temporary basis, may not always be a safe or comfortable place. The homes where foster care kids reside are led by guardians who are almost 50 percent more likely to have gone without work the previous year. These are the residences the system is willingly sending our children. To add to the demoralizing numbers, O'Hare stated only 56 percent of all householders with foster care children in the home worked full time in the previous year. A financial burden may not be something a child feels directly the way a parent does; however, the stress and disadvantages trickle down causing parental withdrawal in communication, affection, and involvement. Financial stress can also lead to parental outbursts and blame shifting, even verbal abuse. Children may see an obvious difference in the material things they own or have at their disposal and what others have, and this can cause a direct stress in the child's life.

These facts are saddening for the children who are in the system; yet most cannot conceptualize the implications of them. The report pointed out that the 700,000 children who passed through the foster care system in Fiscal Year 2000 was the equivalent of one percent of all American children.

Furthermore, the study's analysis discovered "that about 5 percent of the children born in 1990 had experienced foster care by the time they were 15 years old." These statistics show that just because a child enters the foster care system does not mean he or she stays there. It may also mean that a child may be in and out of the system a number of times over the course of his or her childhood.

Within the foster care system, children are assigned different goals according to their originating home situation, age, and other factors. One of those goals is adoption. In 1999, the Administration of Children & Families reports that 128,980 had a goal of adoption, but only 46,870 were actually adopted with public child welfare agency involvement. Since 2000 the number of children adopted from the foster care system has been sitting just above 50,000, not even half of the population of children waiting to be adopted. On September 30, 2009, 114,556 children had a goal of adoption. Of those, 22 percent, or 24,773 children, had been waiting in continuous foster care for 3 to nearly 5 years. The average wait in continuous foster care for the entire group in waiting was 3 years and 2 months found by AFCARS Report of September 2009. A child changes so much in three years physically, mentally, spiritually, and socially. It is during childhood that a person learns the nature of a family, and many times fostered children loose pivotal opportunity to understand love and gain personal growth. They are rejected in heart, often learning only what those lonely years teach them.

It is almost an embarrassment to hear about the number of children who sit unclaimed, while thousands of parents in the nation are unable to get pregnant and so desperately want to. It is a popular trend to go to the fertility clinic and spend thousands of dollars trying to have a baby of your own. Even generic domestic adoptions cost thousands of dollars, and international ones cost more dollars than that, years of waiting, and usually much added stress. All of these are noble in action, faith, and effort, and I applaud all who go forward to gain the things the Lord has spoken each couple to do. Here is another open door for those who did not know of this opportunity and who have a heart to move upon it.

The AFCARS Report showed 57,466 children were adopted in Fiscal Year 2009. The age adopted of highest percentage was 2 years. A total of 8,366 two year olds were adopted that year. While two year olds made up 20 percent of the total foster care population in 2009, the 15-17 year old age group made up 24 percent, nearly one quarter of the foster care population. While adoption is the objective of one type of case goal, there are several others that must be brought to attention to explain the high percentage of teenagers.

One case goal in foster care is reunification with family. This means that the workers deem the situation can be rectified and that the family can become stable enough to support the life of a child in a healthy manner. Another type of goal is adoption. That is easy enough to understand. This means the original guardian's rights have been relinquished and the child needs a new stable permanent home. Another goal is long-term foster care. This means the child's case has no goal for a permanent family and is sometimes geared towards remaining in a residential or group home setting. The last case goal addressed here is emancipation, which means the child's goal is to grow up in and exit out of the foster care system as an 18 year old adult. While 25 percent of the children in foster care polled on September 30, 2009, had a goal of adoption, 8 percent had a goal of long term foster care, and 6 percent had a goal of emancipation. The last two case goals make up 14 percent, or 58,908 kids, whose files have emblematically written on paper 'no hope for a family' and a 'bleak future'. It is a despair and disappointment that these children live knowing the system encourages no one to make them a part of any family home. Instead, they are meant to continue to be a ward of the state – nobody's child.

Regardless of the goal assigned, many children do "age out" of the system, reaching the age of legal adulthood and no longer upheld with any support by government or otherwise. The AFCARS Report in 2009 showed a breakdown of all the reasons and numbers for children exiting the foster care system. Some were reunified with parents. Some were adopted, but 11 percent were emancipated. That was 29, 471 children left to their own devises of survival, some never allowed to return to their foster parents again due to legalities. That correlates very well with the all 18 year olds who exited out of the system the same year, totaling 26,416 young adults. The discrepancy in numbers is found mostly in each state's definition of adulthood used for foster care emancipation.

In 2007, Jim O'Hara, managing director of health and human services for The Pew Charitable Fund said that 67 more young people were "aging out" of the foster care system every day. The issue has become a growing concern in recent years among those in the system. In fact, teens aging out of foster care grew 41 percent in less than one decade, from 1998 to 2007. Ten states in 2007 had more than 10 percent of their total foster care population age out (The Pew Charitable Trust, Miller, 2007).

A report in 2007 called "Time for Reform: Aging out and On Their Own" by the Jim Casey Youth Opportunities Initiative and Kids Are Waiting group found some crucial and intimidating facts about kids who age out. One in four will be incarcerated within the first two years after they have left the system. Over 20% will experience homelessness at some point after age 18, and while 87 percent of the general population holds a high school diploma by age 19, only 58 percent of aged out youth do. By the time they are 25 years old, only 3 percent have a college degree, while 28 percent of the general population does. Statistically, aged-out youth do not have much to look forward to. The numbers consistently run against them and their future.

The study prudently stated, "Foster youth are no more ready for "independence" at age 18 than their non-foster care peers." It is true that almost all parents will spend some money and most will spend thousands of dollars on their children after age 18 on items like helping with occasional bills, rent, college tuition and expenses, car purchases, car maintenance, food, etc. (Ask an empty nester what their list looks like, and you'll get a more personal touch of reality.) The average amount spent by parents after age eighteen is $44,500 (Time for Reform). It is no wonder that these young adults end up homeless or in jail trying to make ends meet in illegal acts. In addition, parents supply emotional support in times of stress, decision-making, and life difficulties. The family of origin is a place of refuge young adults utilize until they have fully established themselves. Even through adulthood holidays and celebrations are an assumed gathering of family.

Nicole, a former foster youth in Oregon, said in the Time for Reform report, "I turned 18 a month before I graduated from high school. The day after graduation, I was kicked out of my foster home, where I had been living for two years. I was 18, a high school graduate on my way to college in the fall, and I was homeless." What a devastating picture of a young woman who was ambitious enough to go for the odds and strive for college, all the while being stripped of support to help her maintain a normal living and the means to achieve her life goals.

Josh, another former foster youth from Oregon said, "It is the end of my first term in college. All the students here talked about how they went home and spent time with their families during Christmas break. When they asked me what I did, I said I slept and wished that my family would come back to me. All I ever wanted was to be able to spend time with my family. I wanted to have someone tell me 'I love you' so much and 'I believe in you.'" Can your imagination draw up a picture of little to no support, no family, and nowhere to turn to for love? I wish I could just take up pages and pages to show you all the quotes that are bundled up in this heart wrenching report. One girl who aged out of the system talks about wanting to have a dad walk her down the aisle one day when she gets married and have grandparents to her children. Another youth talks about the relentless desire to just have a lifelong mentor, someone they can always talk to even through all the inconsistencies of the system. Another young adult talks about having to deal with very deep and stressful subjects on his own because the foster parent never listened. Another aged out youth says "they just randomly move you" from home to home and speaks of the insecurity that develops thereafter.

There is something we as Christians can do to make a difference. It is much more than a cup of cold water, although you will end up doing that if you bring one of these children into your home. This is a growing generation of the forgotten, downtrodden and hopeless, and the number of this group is only increasing in size. But there are many a child in the foster care system from infant to age 18 who want a mother, a father, and a family forever. A good beginning resource for adopting from the foster care system is www.adoptuskids.org. There they display a wonderful layout of children who are looking for homes. Each child has a personal description and photograph. Many come from families and may include 2, 3, 4, 5, or 6 siblings who in many instances are looking for placement in the same home in order to stay together. It is so important to keep the children intact and in the same family home. The Lord may place on your heart to adopt just one or to adopt 6 and keep the siblings who need one another desperately in one unit.

As I looked at the website home page some time ago, Mashach, 16, of Pennsylvania, was the featured child. His description says he makes friends easily and has many at school and in the neighborhood he is in. I searched for him again before publishing this book and much to the breaking of my heart, I think I have found the same young man still listed, this time 17 years old. It pains me to know that he is all too close to aging out. There is also a group of six siblings aged 1 to 9 from California who are looking for a home where they can all stay together. To quote the website caption: "Ashton, Beau, Brittnay, Drew, Brant, and Ernie are in need of a stable, loving nurturing forever family who will adore and welcome them into their home." As I view the webpage, there are currently 3,687 cases on the website of children in need of a home and who are available for adoption. All of them can be viewed on the website, most with pictures and detailed descriptions of the children's personality, along a listing of location, age and gender. This is so different than a $25,000 domestic adoption or a five year-in-waiting international adoption. Adopting a child at this point in the journey while their file is still geared toward finding a permanent home is the point of decreasing the number of children who age out of the system. Let's put a stop to the trend of raising children without parents, and let's bring them in by the willing Spirit of God. Come halt the title "fatherless generation", and teach them the ways of love and inclusion. If you have a heart to take in and rescue a teen whose file has been marked "emancipation" and set them up for infinite orphan-hood, contact your local or state foster care agency and persist in finding what you're looking for.

Besides viewing the website, you can also call AdoptUsKids directly at 1-888-200-4005. A second resource is Heart Gallery of America. Professional photographers volunteer their time and talent to capture these children in a beautiful light, exuding the unique personality of each one. There is a chapter of the Heart Gallery for nearly every state, and they can be found online at www.heartgalleryofamerica.org. In general it takes about 12 months to adopt a child from the time the process is initiated. Although there are significant amounts of paperwork and classes to attend, the most amazing part of this is that most adoptions from foster care are nearly free. Some minimal fees may incur depending on the agency used, but overall, this is an opportunity that will allow you to love a child without a pressing financial barrier.

Many children are in desperate need of a loving family. Each age group comes with its own unique needs, but every person regardless of age needs the nurturing care of a family. Even adults who have never known love or unconditional support have need to feel that for the first time. For the same reason people get connected in a church and gain the support of a team around them, a child needs his or her own support team, one who will teach the child that he or she is important and loved by a holy God. I believe God is sending something specific in this generation. I believe he is looking down on those who know Him and is wooing them to the Spirit of Adoption. I believe He is asking us to pour out His love as best we can in the way He pours out His love on us.

CHAPTER

11

Elijah is Coming

"We are going to be part of an Elijah revolution that can overthrow the altars of Baal [and] then release the hearts of the fathers to the children!!" In 2010, Lou Engle said these words in a conference in Austin as he taught on The Doctrine of the Shedding of Innocent Blood. Oh, how the Israelites worshipped Baal and worshipped Molech by killing their children. Every altar was covered in the blood of innocent children or smoldering with the smoke of infants' burned flesh. It was a stench that would move God to action. He called out with the words in the mouths of the prophets. 'How dare you take human lives that I dreamed up and preciously decorated with my workmanship? Who are you to say that what I have created is nothing but food for a lifeless god?' Today He might say it is fuel for the enemy.

Killing children is an act of worship to selfishness among other little gods. Abandoning them is an act of the same. Ignoring that it happened perpetuates the sin. Just like Israel set up physical alters to idols in their day, we are setting up spiritual ones in our hearts. Lou said that the altars to Baal can be torn down again this time in our world, and there is one way to do it. We have to confront the false idol. One man of God did so directly. Elijah showed himself to the King of Israel during a time when he, Elijah, was the most wanted man in the land. He told King Ahab, 'Bring me all of Israel, we'll see whose God is real.' His confrontation was no experiment, God sent Elijah to prove to the people who He was. The two sides built their altars. The prophets of Baal built their altar to Baal and prayed for him to send fire from heaven to burn up the sacrifice they laid out for him. Two hours later there was nothing. Three hours later Baal didn't show. Four and possibly five hours later, Elijah raised his voice to the people. He couldn't take their dancing, whooping and hollering, or their bloody self mutilation any more. He asked the people to come see his God show up.

Elijah prepared an altar to the Lord God and laid the sacrifice upon it. He dug out a tunnel around the altar. He poured bucket after bucket of water over the altar until it was completely drenched and sitting in a thick pool of water as if to smoother any trust of Baal in the hearts of the indignant. Before he called out to God to send flames from heaven and lick up the sacrifice, he asked the Lord in a simple prayer not to fail him in this great moment "so these people will know that you, LORD, are God, and that you are turning their hearts back again" (1 Kings 18:37, NIV). Of course, after he prayed God showed up. Fire licked up the sacrifice – altar and all, even the pool of water. The prophets of Baal ran away like madmen, were taken over by the Israelites, and killed at Elijah's command.

The story is a great one retold again and again by teachers and pastors. They talk about the power of God and the robust confidence of Elijah. I have heard the miracle lifted up as the gold nugget of the story in sermon after sermon, but I don't think the point of all that had anything to do with miracle power. Its purpose was not for amusement or entertainment satisfaction. Elijah's boldness allowed God to do the work he desired, but the work He desired was not to put on a show. It was to win the heart of his people once again. After the contest of prophets had ended and "When all the people saw this, they fell prostrate and cried, "The LORD—he is God! The LORD—he is God!"" (1 Kings 18:39, NIV). God had turned the hearts of the people to himself. His mission in that moment was accomplished in compassion. The altars made to Baal in the hearts of his people were indeed annihilated, and Elijah's confrontation made allowance for it.

Charles Swindoll wrote a book about a decade ago called Elijah: A man of Heroism and Humility. He takes the reader verse by verse through the prophet's life. Each chapter is an unfolding event or defining time with which Swindoll applies to our own lives. He writes about the sheer heroism imbedded in the man's name.

> "The first thing that commands our attention is Elijah's name. The Hebrew word for "God" in the old testament is *Elohim*, which is occasionally abbreviated *El*. The word *jah* is the word for "Jehovah." Thus, in Elijah's name we find the word for "God" and the word for "Jehovah." Between them is the small letter I, which in Hebrew has reference to the personal pronoun 'my' or 'mine." Putting the three letters together then, we find that Elijah's name means "My God is Jehovah" or "The Lord is my God."" (12)

Whenever Elijah came to someone perhaps introducing himself, it was as though he was trumpeting a mighty stand – The Lord is My God. He didn't care if the friend or foe was for or against God. No, he was announcing the embodiment of his arrival as dedication and loyalty to YHWH. The whisper of his name could have destroyed strongholds and incurred blessing, not because of the man but because of the declaration *in* his name. In his day, he stood before the wiles of evil in the highest places of Israel's government. In the natural, he couldn't have changed anything, but by the power of the Spirit of God in him, he was sent to challenge the enemy's infiltration in the hearts of His people.

In the gospel of Luke many generations later, this spirit is mentioned before Jesus in full ministry comes on scene. While Zechariah, the father of John the Baptist, is fulfilling his duty to serve a highly honored task in the temple, an angel appears to him. The angel comes to tell him that he will have a son with his wife Elizabeth. God has a mandate for John, and the angel goes on to tell what it is (Luke 1:16-17, NIV).

> He will bring back many of the people of Israel to the Lord their God. And he will go on before the Lord, in the spirit and power of Elijah, to turn the hearts of the parents to their children and the disobedient to the wisdom of the righteous—to make ready a people prepared for the Lord.

In the first line, the angel describes the general commission over John's life. The thesis is that God wants the people to come back to Him. He desires that they turn to him and worship Him and Him alone. The second part describes the how. Verse seventeen says that John will be in the spirit and power of Elijah. Elijah had a great boldness within him that was required in order to do the things God told him to do. Elijah also had a great compassion as seen in his prayer on Mount Carmel for his own people. The last part is the fulfilling of what that power and spirit will do. He says that John will "turn the hearts of the parents to their children and the disobedient to the wisdom of the righteous". It makes sense almost immediately that if God wants to bring a nation back to himself that he would release wisdom. The Israelites gained wisdom the day they saw no power come out from Baal but a mighty power come down from Jehovah. Truly the Israelites feared for their lives when they saw God send a fury of a fire out of now where to prove Himself. Their honor shifted to heaven. Proverbs 9:10 says the fear of the Lord is the beginning of wisdom. If we are going to obey and love our God we must have knowledge of Him and His ways.

What does turning parents' hearts have to do with anything? Well, it is a heart change for one; God cannot use hardened hearts. Only a soft heart can be utilized. God needs a tender and pliable heart of man to accomplish His will. As real hearts turn to God, they will turn to the places God's heart sends. Secondly, it is an expression of love, and we know that God is the essence of love. So loving anyone is an expression of God. Remembering several chapters back, the first commandment in Deuteronomy was addressed. We know the first commandment is to LOVE the Lord your God with all your heart, mind, soul, and strength. The scriptural development of that thought in Deuteronomy led to teaching the next generation, the continuation of godliness. The generation that did not receive the Lord's teaching, commandments, and miracle stories were the ones who were led astray. These were the children who grew up and did not know the Lord. But if God were to bring people back to Himself, He would turn the hearts of the believing moms and dads to the children in order for teaching, loving, rearing, instructing, storytelling, and testimonies to breakthrough! This is the power that can bring the children to Himself.

The why is revealed, but its revelation in Luke's context is limited for application to us in modern times. God says that He wanted to do this because He wanted "to make ready a people prepared for the Lord". The most obvious understanding is that John the Baptist stood as the forerunner for the entrance of the Messiah. The Most High anointed John to do the work of "preparing the way" for God to come as a man so that the gospel could come forth and reap a successful harvest. Just as seed is sown in the ground, Jesus said words are sown in the heart, but only fertile soil that is made ready will bring a good crop. John was the farmer tilling the ground in the spirit of Elijah, making ready men's hearts to receive the One who was on the brink of going public. So what does that mean for us today?

The scripture and context found in Malachi 4 brings the greater revelation. This short chapter describes the last day. This is God's day, also known as the day when God's judgment and wrath are released into the earth. The chapter illustrates how it is a fearful day for the wicked but a day of redemption for those who believe. God finishes the chapter with these last two verses (5-6, NKJ):

> "Behold, I will send you Elijah the prophet
> Before the coming of the great and dreadful day of
> the LORD.
> And he will turn

The hearts of the fathers to the children,
And the hearts of the children to their fathers,
Lest I come and strike the earth with a curse."

The angel who spoke to Zechariah was speaking about this truth but in a different manner. God said in the first scripture that John was coming in the Spirit of Elijah. This scripture states emphatically that the prophet Elijah is coming himself, and Elijah will be showing up on the front steps of the world's stage only prior to "the great and dreadful day of the Lord".

Jesus addressed this subject with a few of his disciples in Matthew 17:10-13. As he talks about the signs of their day, read what he mentions about another day.

> The disciples asked him, "Why then do the teachers of the law say that Elijah must come first?"
> Jesus replied, "To be sure, Elijah comes and will restore all things. But I tell you, Elijah has already come, and they did not recognize him, but have done to him everything they wished. In the same way the Son of Man is going to suffer at their hands." Then the disciples understood that he was talking to them about John the Baptist. (NIV)

The teachers of the law had recognized the truth that Elijah would come before the Messiah did, and Jesus confirms this when he says, "To be sure." It's as if he is saying 'Absolutely, they have that right.' The latter part of Jesus' explanation tells them that Elijah has come prior to His own coming. He was putting the disciples' minds at rest. Yes, indeed the teachers are right, and yes, indeed this is how – John the Baptist was that Elijah. He confirms this more prominently in chapter 11:

11, 13-14. "Truly I tell you, among those born of women there has not risen anyone greater than John the Baptist . . . For all the Prophets and the Law prophesied until John. And if you are willing to accept it, he is the Elijah who was to come." (NIV) This was the point of interest for that generation, and they needed to have full confidence that the scriptures lined up and that they believed in the right man. Jesus reassured them several times over.

However, there is another context in Jesus' speech to the disciples. Let's read Matthew 17:11 again. "Jesus replied, "To be sure, Elijah comes and will restore all things"" (NIV). Before Jesus goes on to explain the past tense of the already established John the Baptist, He speaks in present and future tense. "Elijah comes" is a present tense that I believe encompasses more than just the current present but it establishes an existence. Elijah came in the Old Testament and restored some things in his day in Israel. The spirit of Elijah showed up in John the Baptist to restore the hearts of the men in preparation for the Messiah. Elijah will come to prepare the second coming of Jesus when He will appear in all glory and make all things new. Elijah comes. I can say the future tense with confidence because Jesus does so in that same sentence, "Elijah . . . *will* restore all things."

Oh! That must be a misinterpretation, a mistranslation, right? I think it is perfectly correct. If Jesus is going to come again, why wouldn't Elijah come again? Besides, John the Baptist is already beheaded at this point. He is formally and knowingly deceased in chapter 14, and yet our bibles have printed unapologetically in chapter 17 that Elijah will restore. Jesus' first appearance on earth was not the fulfillment of the great and dreadful day of the Lord. He did not judge in that time span. He came as a mercy ship. He came as the lamb. That was not the Lord's Day of Judgment, and on that day He will resemble more readily the lion. Yet Malachi says that just before Judgment Day, Elijah shows up. For the day that we have yet to see Jesus fulfill, we have yet to see Elijah fulfill.

The prophet is coming to make hearts come in compassion to one other. This time it is more than a one way street. In Luke, the word spoke directly of the release of the fathers' hearts to the children. This time God is not just anointing one side but he is anointing two sides: the fathers and the children. With this anointing there will be a harvest of children's hearts that turn to their fathers. This translates into something powerful when taken into consideration. The Lord is anointing adults to have compassion for children and the next generation, and this anointing *is* the Spirit of Adoption. If you are seeking the Lord, you do not have to try to "get" this anointing or desire the Lord is sending out. It will overtake you. What is most profound is that He is anointing the hearts of children today who are now without the Holy Spirit and the Word of the Lord to receive a heart to turn to you who know the Lord that they might be a recipient of everlasting life.

Why does God want us to continue in that mindset with a heart turned to our kids? Loving children is most obviously a good thing. Jesus himself did that by holding young ones and blessing them as recorded in scripture. He also said, "Whoever welcomes one of these little children in my name welcomes me" (Mark 9:37, NIV). Preparing their hearts to receive God's heart is a righteous work. Lou Engle tells of a dream he had one night where the Lord gave him the verses in Luke 1 concerning John the Baptist coming in the spirit of Elijah. "As I woke up from the dream, the Lord spoke resoundingly to my heart "What I am pouring out in America is stronger than the rebellion"" (Nazarite DNA). The spirit of Elijah and this beautiful entanglement with the Father's heart - the Spirit of Adoption - is the solution to overcoming our nation's current disobedience.

I think it is clear, this spirit and anointing once released by God's plan and design for the first coming of the Messiah will show up again this time manifested in the latter appearance of Elijah at crucial God-hours just before the second coming. He is preparing his people for the coming of the Lord. As we approach our King's second coming in all His glory, He will send out His anointing for the soil to be tilled once again. He wants to bring His people back to Himself. This call will only expand in time and space and intensify as we approach the day. God will not draw back; He will only increase the shout like one who shouts in the wilderness. "Clear the way through the wilderness for the Lord! Make a straight highway through the wasteland for our God!" (Isaiah 40:3) His appeal to our spirits will not die down, unless we choose to shut our ears to His word. God has enlisted His chosen to do the work He requires before He makes His final entry.

The Spirit of Adoption persists in so many situations and needs. It is the thread that enables love. It is the language that says "I am for you, not against you." It is the destroyer of unhealthy independence and self neglect. I beckon you to consider what God is saying to you as you read these words. Where is He calling this placement of the Spirit of Adoption in your life? Is it to first grow deeper in relationship with Him, to know that you are completely His? You may find you need personal restoration and inner healing, understanding your parents are not the perfect image of God if their memories are what pains you. God will allow you to love them because he created them flesh and soul; and He loves them just as He created you and loves you. Perhaps this call is to engage you in the children of your own family and halt the abandonment that is decaying the relationships in your home. Perhaps you are ready to step into a mentor roll in the church looking for hungry teens who are first generation Christians with no immediate and constant source of help to turn to. However, the Lord may call you to meet the needs of little children, who are not yours, in your very home. You did not bring the child into the world nor suffer the labor pains, but you may get to see the fruit of their life blossom through a selfless act of obedience and love. And perhaps by your act of love, you will see them accept the invitation to heaven. John 4:35b, 37-38 (NIV) says,

> "I tell you, open your eyes and look at the fields! They are ripe for harvest . . . Thus the saying 'One sows and another reaps' is true. I sent you to reap what you have not worked for. Others have done the hard work, and you have reaped the benefits of their labor."

May this word blossom with the heart of the Father in you.

King Herod's Decree

I received a vision of great personal revelation one night from the Lord. I was at a night revival and prayer meeting south of New Orleans in a small church called World Prayer Tabernacle. The Lord was moving. People were walking up to the front to receive healings. I really hadn't felt much power in the worship that night; although, I know many other people had. I was trying to press into the Spirit, but I wasn't getting what I had anticipated. At the end of the service during the alter call, the Lord began talking to me. It wasn't so much what I saw as it was the implications that really affected me. I understood there was a powerful destiny for God's people and a powerful reproach from the enemy. It shook my insides and made my soul a passionate force pleading with God to do something. After the service, I penned the vision the Lord gave me.

> Journal Entry November 10, 2010: "The Lord said
> He would lift up America . . . He told me to see the
> children, to look at the children. To raise up the

next generation. Something about saving America is saving the babes and small children or the other way around, but it's not what I was originally thinking. I imagined saving adults and bringing them back to Christ, but I saw children that when God said to save America he was talking about souls, unborn babies who proclaim His name. Children. I just saw a bunch of them [staring right back at me with "help" written in the listless expressions of their faces]. And I saw children in the womb, embryos in the sack that Satan was trying to attack and shake. He, Satan, was trying to get his hands on these embryos and kill them."

The devil does not want anyone going to heaven. He is jealous that we are called "the apple of his eye". He does not want Christ to be revealed in anyone's heart, let alone all the earth. He does not want Christ to receive His inheritance, the church. It so happens that God the Father will be giving Jesus the Messiah a place of rulership and an iron scepter while He sits at God's right hand. These are some of the very things the devil wanted for Himself, and in due process of giving over to the lusts of his pride and acting out in rebellion, he lost all of these things and any place in heaven. Jesus, however, is yoked up and one with God. He is in perfect relationship with Him, something the devil will never have.

When the Lord moves in power, Satan is right there ready to pounce on any opportunity to destroy what heaven is building. The single most powerful event of all human history is when God Himself came in the form of man, and His rival enemy was on the move and alert. Satan would by all means never want to sit idle while God moves, especially not when he is hearing of his own impending destruction. Isaiah had prophesied that "to us a child is born, to us a son is given, and the government will be on His shoulders" (Isaiah 9:6a NIV). The same prophet also proclaimed "Of the greatness of His government and peace there will be no end. He will reign on David's throne and over his kingdom, establishing and upholding it with justice and righteousness from that time on and forever" (Isaiah 9:7a-b NIV). This meant not just that someone would arise, but that He would be over all of earth's government. Beyond that it would be of the same kingdom as King David's, and this reign would never end. To the rival enemy, Satan, this meant his employment as prince of the air would soon be quenched.

He knew this was the time the messiah was coming. Satan could sense the vibrations in the air, the excitement in heaven. He may have been witness to the angels who appeared before Mary or Joseph. He might have seen the wise men bow down to the child in the stable. I am sure powers of darkness were made well known of the angels who sang in chorus to the Lord of hosts the night the Messiah was born. He might have understood better than the people of the day what those words Isaiah spoke had meant. Satan was nervous that this might be God's desired time for the prophecies of an earthly ruler from the line of David to come to fruition. So, the enemy of darkness devised a plan that would surely take out the Son of God. Knowing the Lord was on His way, the devil sent out a particular strategy, an articulate thought through a powerful man, King Herod. He stirred it up in Herod's heart to kill every male child two years old and younger in the city of Bethlehem where he heard the infant king was residing.

Satan was jealous and reviled at the Lord's plans. His goal was to stop the Lord from ever coming. In effort to stop the birth of a new covenant and the release of love to all men, he meant to abort the Lord's design before it should arise. We know now that what is intended for Christ's second coming is not what was planned for His first. His first coming brought salvation to all men, making the invitation to join his family. His second coming will bring his family into the dwelling of the new heaven and the new earth, and he will arise as king over it. Because the enemy cannot know everything, his efforts are often not as direct or effective as the Lord's, and he doesn't care who gets taken out in the process. He throws a sword in every direction until his goal is won. Such reckless release of ammunition for the life of one person sends a picture much like a madman on a machine gun. Satan festered with anger that released wicked acts in indiscriminate measure. He didn't stop at killing just one child, he would take all the Jewish sons down with the Son of God. The enemy was handing out no mercy for any son to escape his wrath.

Although Satan's strategy at the birth of Jesus did not win him any advancement or halt God's will, Satan is not so despondent in one defeat that he has given up his fight. There is yet to be a government on Jesus' shoulders (Isaiah 9:6), established justice in the earth (Isaiah 9:7), and a new heaven and a new earth (Rev. 21:1). The first of Isaiah 9:6 has come to pass: "to us a child is born, to us a son is given". But the last part is yet to be fulfilled: "and the government will be on his shoulders". In accompaniment to this, John's revelation after Christ's resurrection revealed that Satan's doom is still lurking when he will be bound for a thousand years in the Abyss (Rev.

20:2-3) and ultimately thrown into the lake of fire (Rev. 20:10). The end of his own freedom and position may be most alarming to Satan. In the vision that John saw while he was on the isle of Patmos, there was an angel from heaven "having the key to the Abyss and holding in his hand a great chain. He seized the dragon, that ancient serpent, who is the devil, or Satan, and bound him for a thousand years. He threw him into the Abyss, and locked and sealed it over him . . ." (Rev 20:1b-3a, NIV). Because of this prophecy, Satan is warring against Jesus' final return and more furiously than ever (Rev. 12:12).

The disciples asked Jesus what would be the sign of His return, the second coming. He said among many things that there would be wars and rumors of wars. Nation would rise against nation, and there are would be famines and earthquakes around the world (Matthew 24). Of course none of these specify to us exactly what time we are looking at, only that we are getting closer to His arrival, which is always true as long as the sun is rising and setting. Two points of interest in His discourse draw us in closer. First, He says that there will be an increase of wickedness and because of this wickedness the love of most will grow cold (Matt 24:12). Opposite to many Christians' interpretations of this scripture, Jesus is talking about believers. It isn't an unbeliever's heart who doesn't know agape love that grows cold. Who else would have true love that could grow cold? Only a person who has the love of God in him has the opportunity to lose that love and turn a bitter route. Take note of everything around you, and keep yourself from the dimming grays that fade out your zeal for the Lord. See if you notice this happening around you or perhaps in larger contexts of Christians in the public eye. A very urgent and real charge to the church today is Proverbs 4:23: Guard your heart for it is the wellspring of life.

The second astonishing point Jesus makes is that the gospel will be preached to the whole world! And at that, then the end will come. (Matt 24:14) Some measurable data for current times is available for this last note. According to the Joshua Project, of the 6.75 billion people on earth, almost 3 billion are still void of ever hearing the gospel (Joshua Project, Statistics pg). Most of these people are in what is commonly referred to as the 10/40 window, meaning the countries and people groups between 10 and 40 degrees longitude. Although the 10/40 window is a difficult area to penetrate because of the vast numbers of languages and cultures, the unreached people within it encompass a little more than 40% of the world's total population. That means over half of the world, almost 60%, has heard the gospel. Whether this mission will be a slow battle or a quick flooding of evangelical Christians is partially up to our response. However, it turns out we know that we can evaluate current standing by collected data of the unified church. One thing we do know is that we are to be sober and fully alert. Jesus said at the end of the discussion "Therefore keep watch, because you do not know on what day your Lord will come" (Matthew 24:42 NIV).

Hypothetically speaking, where and how would Satan begin to halt something like this, especially when the day and the hour are unknown, even to Jesus? Just like he did with the first coming, he will look into the book of the prophets and listen to the prophecies of the present day. He is listening conspicuously for God's hints. The devil is not by any means all knowing, but he is perceptive, and he is roaming the earth. He has his antennas on, and he is looking for key words and phrases. This is the same thing he did at Jesus' first coming. He probably heard the prophecy's given by Anna and Simeon when the infant, Jesus, was brought to the temple for circumcision. Satan knows the prophets hear from God. So he listens close to get his best game plan. He, too, was looking for the fulfillment of the word of Isaiah about a prince of peace coming and acted upon it.

If we look into scripture, beyond the terrors that speak of the last days, we focus in on what Satan is looking for. He wants to discover a prophetic event meant for the future that God will perform as a precursor to the coming of our Lord, Jesus Christ. If he can stop the precursor, he might be able to halt the event. The one item that stands out from the rest is quoted twice in scripture. That, my friends, is a highlight in the devil's checklist. The prophet Joel wrote a short but powerful testimony to the Lord about the last days. Late in chapter 2 Joel speaks this as the voice piece for the Lord:

> "And afterward,
>   I will pour out my Spirit on all people.
> Your sons and daughters will prophesy,
>   your old men will dream dreams,
>   your young men will see visions.
> Even on my servants, both men and women,
>   I will pour out my Spirit in those days.
> I will show wonders in the heavens
>   and on the earth,
>   blood and fire and billows of smoke.
> The sun will be turned to darkness
>   and the moon to blood
>   before the coming of the great and dreadful day
> of the LORD." (Joel 2:28-31 NIV)

We know that these scriptures are speaking of the last days because verse 31 says that it this pouring out will come before "the great and dreadful day of the Lord." The next chapter immediately talks about the judgment of the nations. The Lord says that He is going to gather all the nations so that He can enter into judgment against them (Joel 3:2).So right before the Lord is ready to pour out His wrath, an act of mercy and of power takes place. He pours out his Spirit on all His people. It is by His Spirit that the miraculous takes place. Even in this passage, there will be dreams and visions of the Lord given by His Spirit. Paul speaks about a wide range of gifts that Christians have from wisdom to faith to miraculous powers, and he says, "All these are the work of one and the same Spirit, and He distributes them to each one, just as He determines" (1 Corinthians 12:11 NIV). These are gifts that were operating even in the first century church, and the Lord utilized the gifts of his people so often that the supernatural became expected among Christians.

A man of the first century church named Peter quotes this exact excerpt from Joel as the preemptive opener in his pioneer sermon against shouts of indictment on the day of Pentecost. No one considered what these new believers were experiencing and expressing was from the Spirit of God. They believed the men were drunk, only making fools out of themselves. Peter knew what he was experiencing was of God, and he knew that there was great power in it. He saw a fulfillment of an old prophecy in the scriptures. In explaining the first move of the power of the Holy Spirit to the skeptical passer-byers at Pentecost, he says:

These men are not drunk, as you suppose. It's only
nine in the morning! No, what you see was predicted
long ago by the prophet Joel:
'In the last days,' God says,
   'I will pour out my Spirit upon all people.
Your sons and daughters will prophesy.
   Your young men will see visions,
   and your old men will dream dreams.
In those days I will pour out my Spirit
   even on my servants—men and women alike—
   and they will prophesy.
And I will cause wonders in the heavens above
   and signs on the earth below—
   blood and fire and clouds of smoke.
The sun will become dark,
   and the moon will turn blood red
   before that great and glorious day of the LORD arrives.
But everyone who calls on the name of the LORD
   will be saved.' (Acts 2:15-21 NIV)

The outcome of this event was the salvation of 3,000 souls.
The power of God in the anointing of the Holy Spirit broke out
and a new wave of believers spread like wildfire. Those who
were first accusing the men and the Holy Spirit soon became
witness to those who would turn and believe in it. It was an
immediate addition to the body of Christ! But it was by the
power of the Holy Spirit that such a mighty event occurred.
Even though this was a fulfillment of scripture from the minor
prophet, it was merely a partial fulfillment. The clarification
here is in the fact that this event in the book of Acts was not
directly before the "great and glorious day of the Lord." The
Lord is still coming, and he is still waiting patiently for his

final appearance to earth as we know it. But the tilling of the hearts that must happen before Christ's second return will be a mighty one. We are looking forward to a generation that will have the call of John the Baptist with the power of God's Spirit. This is going to be a greater outpouring than we or any other generation has seen before because we must harvest a greater number of souls than we have ever harvested before.

God has promised through His prophet Joel and reminded us again through Peter that a day is coming when He will be pouring out the Spirit on every person who will receive it, and with that Spirit comes great signs and wonders that will save multitudes, just like the effects of the signs and wonders at Pentecost brought a mass of hearts into the dwelling place of God. You see, many believed Jesus because of the miracles that followed Him. John wrote in his gospel, "Now while [Jesus] was in Jerusalem at the Passover Festival, many people saw the signs He was performing *and believed in His name*" (John 2:23, NIV). Some men will believe because of the words that are preached, but others will be won to the faith because of the signs they see that only God could perform.

The story of Thomas is a wonderful display of the power of miracles and the supernatural. After Jesus had died many of the disciples had seen the risen Christ and were full of joy and excitement, but Thomas was not there when Jesus appeared. His personal pain and grief probably led him in cautious skepticism. A downcast heart in Thomas due to Jesus' death may have wounded his faith in ways that he didn't know how to escape.

So the other disciples told him, "We have seen the Lord!" But he [Thomas] said to them, "Unless I see the nail marks in his hands and put my finger where the nails were, and put my hand into his side, I will not believe." (John20:25, NIV)

Thomas was committed to disbelief until he was witness to the other disciple's claims. One week later Jesus appeared, and He met Thomas face to face among the disciples. Because Thomas needed a full validation and lifting up of his faith, Jesus came to him and told him to set his hands exactly where the nails were. Our Lord is so good that he met the demands of a man who would believe in an "only if this" situation. By reading the words of the story, you can feel the heart release that comes over Thomas as he exclaims "My Lord and My God!" (John 20:28b). The supernatural move of God is what moved Thomas to belief. It was because of Jesus' coming in the physical after His death and after His appearance to the others that Thomas could reclaim his faith.

Jesus wants all men to come to Him, and He desires no one to perish (2 Peter 3:9). In doing so He wants to win those who would believe by His word and those who would believe by the supernatural deeds of the Holy Spirit. He desires to reel in the hearts of the doubting Thomases who would otherwise cry out the Lord's name if they could only see their miracle. He is a compassionate God, and because of His passionate obsession with His creation, He is willing to go to great lengths to save as many as will turn to Him. So he endows us with the Holy Spirit to perform the works that He performed on earth and even greater. While Jesus is talking with the disciples, He introduces this concept. Jesus said, "Very truly I tell you, whoever believes in me will do the works I have been doing, and they will do even greater things than these, because I am going to the Father" (John 14:12, NIV). Only sentences later, Jesus presents the idea of the Holy Spirit in verse 16. "And I will ask the Father, and he will give you another advocate to help you and be with you forever."

After Jesus is raised from the dead, He makes Himself known to His disciples. He speaks with them about many things and presents Himself to many people for a total of 40 days. A crux point of direction for the disciples comes at a word before He leaves the earth. He gives them the mantle of the Great Commission, to go into all the earth and preach the gospel. As if without a breath between thoughts, in the very next sentence, Jesus says, "And these signs will accompany those who believe: In my name they will drive out demons; they will speak in new tongues; they will pick up snakes with their hands; and when they drink deadly poison, it will not hurt them at all; they will place their hands on sick people, and they will get well." (Mark 16:17-18, NIV) It is these signs that God intends to lavish on us. As Christians it is not our prerogative to enter into dangerous situations for performance sake, like drinking poison and holding deadly snakes. There is no advocation for it. Rather the sign will be that as we spread the gospel and Satan spreads his "net" to catch us, we will have power to overcome. Each miracle is done with necessity for advancing the gospel. If a snake is in my way and the only way forward is to move it, then I will pick it up and move it. In that illustration, I would assume no injury by the power of the Holy Spirit. It is in His Spirit that these signs are possible, and it is in the last days that God will be reaping a great harvest. It will not be by the word of

God solely that men are saved. No, it will mightily include the signs and wonders of His Spirit.

It will happen according to the prophetic word that God will pour out His Spirit on all flesh. This is how He saved 3,000 men at a time, and perhaps he will save tens of thousands at a time. This is how the great harvest in the kingdom will explode in awe and heaven will be filled with souls. We are looking for millions to receive Him this time. He is bringing about a last generation to begin the task and see to it that the gospel is preached to the whole world. Then the end will come, and Jesus will enter the stage. This is the destruction of Satan, and this last generation who will be the greatest fulfillment of this prophecy is the precursor that Satan is coming to kill. The second half of my journal entry the night the Lord gave me the vision reveals this epiphany. Continuing from where I left off I wrote:

> "It just occurred to me that Satan is trying to kill the most powerful generation in the Lord in these last days. He is trying to wipe out the anointed and the ones the Lord would pour his Spirit on when He pours it out on all flesh. Maybe those children are the ones the Lord wants to use to save this nation. It's like King Herod who killed all the babies when he found out the messiah was born. He tried to kill God's anointed, only this [present assault] is on a much larger scale."

Satan does not know when this last generation will come except by scriptures preceding Joel 2. Joel 2 begins with God's words "after this". Well, after what? God's Spirit is poured out after a great multitude comes to repentance. Verse 12 says, ""Even now," declares the LORD, "return to me with all your heart, with fasting and weeping and mourning."" (NIV) The entire book of Joel is laced with God's call to his own people to come back to His heart and His ways. Once they repent he pours out blessing in the natural, but he also says that he will pour out on them in the spiritual. There is a word circulating and many Americans and Christians are awaiting a great revival which will sweep the earth. It is something that many believe is still to come. The heart cry of repentance is showing up in solemn assemblies, the large gathering of people who are weeping and mourning before him. People are gathering all over the world asking for the Lord's mercy and repenting on behalf of themselves, their cities, their nations, their churches, and their families. These prayer meetings are in large houses of prayer and small houses of prayer. They are in bible studies and home cell groups. They are heard in church congregations and stadiums filled with tens of thousands of Christians. Some are the wailing of one individual.

If God is setting His plan into motion by setting up solemn assemblies and attitudes of repentance to the pave the way for His blessing to then pour out His Spirit on all flesh, how then do you stop this cycle? Can our enemy stop the solemn assemblies? Maybe. Can he steal the blessing of the Lord? Perhaps for a moment, but God would not endure it to remain that way. If Satan could guess about which generation will receive the outpouring of His Spirit, his thoughts are that he might be able to quench this unruly fire of God from arising. In Revelation 12:4 scripture talks about a woman or the church birthing out a child. The enemy is described as "the dragon", and his vengeance on this birth is foul. He is there before the birth takes place. The words read, "The dragon stood in front of the woman who was about to give birth, so that he might devour her child the moment it was born" (NIV). This is the same devise that King Herod used. This dragon wants to devour the plans of God which are instilled in the people of God. He wants to devour our children and the children of the last generations the way he tried to devour Christ and did devour the children of Bethlehem. This word indicates that Satan prepares himself to take out what God plans to birth out.

If we don't see the devil's weapon, we won't know how and when to act. Today, he is using the same call King Herod spoke over a city. It is a call to kill the children, to stop the plan of God while it is still an infant. If he kills heathens along the way, he is fine with it. If he takes the future souls who were meant to be pastors and evangelists, check mark for him. If he kills great men of faith and women with the voice of truth, he has made progress. If he can stop up the souls that would be voice pieces for God and worship leaders and those that would prophecy and do "greater works than these", he has made great success. If he can cleanse the world of those that truly love God, who would receive this great outpouring, then maybe just maybe the enemy will stop his own future demise. Satan is out to annihilate God's rescue of righteousness just like he did 2,000 years ago. He is turning the minds of present day politicians, parents, and future parents to evil through "rational logic" and "rights". There is not just one man who has bought into the lie of Satan this time. The idea ravishes many in our land.

In part one of his schemes, he aims to kill the generation *before* they stand in God's strength. His weapon finds them in the womb. He may not even know exactly which generation it will be, but it does not matter because he has begun to plunder it under the law of the land through Roe v. Wade and has funded that law with our own tax dollars. He is swinging his sword and will take down anyone and any generation that stands close. This is his plan of continual instituted wickedness: abortion. It's a safe guard for him and a devastating assault on us. I do not want our land to be found like the city of Babylon in Revelation. "In her [Babylon] was found the blood of prophets and of God's holy people" (Rev. 18:24a, NIV). Babylon was guilty of killing God's chosen. Even today, where prophets should rise up, Satan is killing. Where God's anointed are coming into the world, Satan stands by ready to draw their blood. As Christ's life was at stake in those early years of King Herod's decree, so are the prophets and the saints of the next generation. King Herod killed one hundred percent of the children in a city. The young people of America born since 1973 are missing roughly 1/3 of their generation to abortion. The rest are the survivors born to parents who didn't bow to the ideology of death.

Part two of the enemy's plans is a death in the spirit. He has led fathers to abandon children. If he cannot kill the child physically, then he will attempt to destroy the child emotionally. The easiest way to do that is to instill in them an orphan-spirit. Once inherited, it becomes generational, and the enemy's one-time attack becomes residual. So our children, our grandchildren, and every generation thereafter are under the attack of Satan and his schemes in order that he might eliminate the promises of God and ultimately overturn the forecast of his own demise. However, the outcome of the devil's plans will not be victory. Our bible gives us the entire script, and we win by the blood of the Lamb and the word of our testimony.

In the days of Christ's birth, God had a defensive that outwitted the enemy and brought him glory. Just before King Herod put the enemy's plan of slaughter in motion, God spoke to Joseph through an angel in a dream. The Lord gave witness to Joseph of an imminent danger that was coming so that he must move diligently according to the Lord's word. "Get up," He said, "take the child and his mother and escape to Egypt. Stay there until I tell you, for Herod is going to search for the child to kill Him." (Matthew 2:13b-c, NIV) Joseph had already come so far in following the Lord and believing the angel that spoke to him on behalf of Mary and the child in her womb. If Joseph had not obeyed the Lord this time or if he had hesitated too long at this call, the enemy could have succeeded, but God trusted Joseph and relied upon him to fulfill His plan. God put his only son in the form of a weak and vulnerable infant in Joseph's hands. The weapon that would break chains of bondage and the salvation for every Gentile and Jew was placed in the care of a common young man. While God could have used something far greater and more secure, he made the choice to turn to Joseph. Like a hero who fulfills the act of rescue, Joseph made the choice to believe God. He escaped with his family and went into Egypt in accordance with the word of the Lord.

As Joseph was carrying his family to safety, the Kingdom of Heaven was arising with the glory of making room for every man to come boldly before the throne of God. It was God's love sickness for His creation that ignited this plan of love. As in every generation He is calling us to fulfill His purposes and asking us if we will take hold of His words and act on the call. A weight was set on Joseph to accomplish the request of the Lord, and although Joseph did not fully understand the significance of his willingness to comply with the heart of God, he understood something of God's plan was at stake. I posit that something of heavenly significance that requires the action of not just one father, but every father, is at stake in our time, too. Greater attack requires greater response from the front lines of the Church. Joseph wasn't called to carry a biological son; he was called to carry God's son. Many children today are called to be sons and daughters of the living God with destinies we cannot fully understand. The kingdom of heaven is at stake, and God is calling out to Joseph in every land from every nation under every government and in every city to take up the burden that was not given to him by nature but by heaven.

The reality of our days is that we are living in the same urgency and under the same kind of attack as Joseph and Mary. Satan through the embodiment of King Herod tried to kill Jesus, who is a promise of God's word and salvation. In doing so he wiped out an entire city of children ages 0-2. The last generation is a result of God's promise and a precursor to the second coming of Jesus Christ when he will rule and reign. Satan wants to destroy God's works so he is aiming to destroy the last generation. In the midst of those days, Mary made a heart decision after receiving her commission. ""I am the Lord's servant", Mary answered. "May it be to me as you have said.""" (Luke 1:38 NIV) Joseph followed the Lord's word in earnest obedience and stood tall without any notation of wavering. The church can only rise up to take our battle when we decide to own the mantle that God is handing to us. We need the faith to believe as Mary believed and the obedience to follow through just as Joseph courageously chose. The power to act is in our hand.

CHAPTER

13

Our Call

Our call as believers is to raise up a next generation of believers, a righteous youth, a passionate childhood who are aflame and come unglued for their God. We are not to live selfishly as this nation has predisposed our 'Christian' minds to think. This life is not for our benefit in items like cars and houses, nice clothes and furniture, or eating out and socializing or spending our social lives on the advancement of climbing the corporate ladder for personal achievement and satisfaction. Is that satisfaction? Will we be satisfied old in our bed, knowing that we made some phenomenal amount of money over the course of our lives? Will establishing a family name in the world of business bring us eternal satisfaction in the end? Perhaps building up some club or organization will have eternal rewards. No, I tell you no! That will not be satisfying. What is satisfying is knowing you contributed to something that means more than you'll ever know and lives longer than you would ever dream of existing on earth in this body. Things, money, businesses, and organizations do not live forever, but people do. Every soul has an eternal reality.

It is not ours to decide whether or not we get to have natural born children. It is not supposed to be under our authority to limit the number of children we have by death or any other means because we feel like having only as many as will serve our needs. But it never was about having our needs met. Christianity . . . we should define that again. Merriam-Webster says it is "the religion derived from Jesus Christ". We are here to serve because He came to serve. We are to rear up a next generation of believers to take on the vision of the Lord and see to it that they execute that vision given to them direct by the Holy Spirit.

Where are your flaming darts? Psalm 127:4 says "Like arrows in the hand of a warrior, so *are* the children of one's youth" (NKJ) Do you have any? Can't get pregnant? You aren't married? You can still raise up the next generation in spite of those conditions. Work in the church nursery. Get involved in the youth group. Mentor the teenagers down the street and invite them over for cookies. Love them. Teach them. Give them your inheritance. Open your heart of wisdom. I can only hope these words don't fall on deaf ears. Where are the fathers and mothers in the spirit? Who will you love and train up in the way they should go? Rise up, oh, men of God! You have a job to do. And it is not just to change the world, but it is to seek to change the hearts of the next generation. That will change the world! I am calling out all parents in the spirit! Come teach. Come pour out your understanding. Come find the young ones who are lost. Please go to the lonely youth, young adults, and newly weds in the church who seek your council. We are looking for you! Be present in this day and age.

I am calling the hearts of the fathers back to the children and the hearts of the children back to the fathers. Hear them when they cry. This *is* the heart of your Father in Heaven. "God made husbands and wives to become one body and one spirit for His purpose – so they would have children who are true to God," Malachi 2:15 NCV. This is the purpose of the Lord, that there would be no generational gap in the spirit. Many Christian couples get married with the intention of fulfilling their purposes, but God says He puts man and woman together for His purposes. If it is for God's purposes that we are united together with our spouse, then we should seek to know what God's purpose is. His purpose was not merely for sexual enjoyment, romance and flowers, or to fulfill the 'next steps' of life; although by nature marriage enjoys these beautiful things. The bible cautions us not to run after the pleasures of this life. In fact, in his second letter to Timothy, Paul said that the last days will be marked with people who run after these things and they will even dress themselves as believers.

> But mark this: There will be terrible times in the last days. People will be lovers of themselves, lovers of money, boastful, proud, abusive, disobedient to their parents, ungrateful, unholy, without love, unforgiving, slanderous, without self-control, brutal, not lovers of the good, treacherous, rash, conceited, lovers of pleasure rather than lovers of God. (2 Timothy 3:1-3)

Let me plead with you on this one point: do not become a lover of yourself. Infatuation with your possessions, your appearance, your success, your accolades, your time, and every inward driven force is the first problem that unleashes the remaining, gradually increasing, wicked attributes in this letter. I for one do not think it is coincidence. If all a person sees is his own world, pride will erupt and the rest is history. There are married people who are indeed lovers of themselves, but God can use the trustworthy heart of a single person to fulfill the demand to worship Him. In the end, if God gives him a wife, he has a ready heart to look after the eternal rewards and skip past the momentary lusts on earth. In the same breath, I want you to know that God can use you and your spouse, even after living years and years for yourself.

The fruit of marriage is to bring forth the next generation of life and to teach them the way of godliness. And we are not to teach just a form of it but the power that the Holy Spirit ushers in behind it. (2 Timothy 3:5) Just as Jesus sent out His disciples in pairs to preach the good news and advance the Kingdom, He put us in pairs, man and woman, so that we can go out in accountability and power and support to show God to the children He gives us. In our selfishness, as Christians especially in America, we have lost so much of our purpose in the Lord, to live as unto the Lord, not to live as unto ourselves. Having children is not meant to be our option, it is meant to be our blessing - our weaponry. Rearing them up in the Lord is supposed to be a goal of our faith.

Proverbs says have your quiver full of them. Send them out to fight against the enemy. The enemy seeks to steal, kill and destroy. He prowls around like a roaring lion seeking to devour who he may. And prowl he does, into homes all across this nation. He steals love from families, destroys marriages, and kills children while they are still in the womb. But the Lord, however, is roaring too. The book of Hosea describes the love God has for Israel, and in this account the Lord says through the prophet that the ones He loves will follow Him and He will roar like a lion (Hosea 11:10a, NIV). "When He roars, His children will come trembling from the west. They will come from Egypt trembling like sparrows, from Assyria, fluttering like doves" (Hosea 11:10b-11a, NIV). You see, there are children who are called of God but are still living in the world, which is representative of Egypt in the aforementioned scripture. These children will know their Maker, and they will be called out of their lifestyles of sin and desperation of loneliness. They may come trembling before God in all His greatness, but it is possible because of God's heart. In verse eight, He says, "My heart is changed within me; all my compassion is aroused" (Hosea 11:8c, NIV). It is because of God's compassion, enough to move into the situation, that He mightily roars a call to compel his children's souls to Himself. It is a roar not heard in the physical, but it is a heart persuasion from Sprit to spirit.

The May 2011 edition of the American Family Association Journal printed its front cover story: "When Christians Adopt It Changes the World". Inside the journalist tells the family story of Paul and Robin Pennington who began a ministry called Hope for Orphans. They desired children, but when pregnancy was no longer an option for them, they turned to adoption. They raised six children, five of which are adopted, and have ten grandchildren. Robin told of the process behind the family's making. "Initially adopting the first two was to *have* a family.

Then we started really having an ache for the orphan and the child that needed a family. So our second three really came out of a desire to *give a child* a family . . . They are all our real children. God brought some through adoption and some through biological means, but before the foundations of the earth they were all ours."

God has an ultimate destination for these children. He doesn't intend to call and leave the task undone. No, He is like the Good Samaritan that told the innkeeper to look after him because He was returning for the unwanted heart. In the last portion of the last verse of this section in Hosea, God gives His reason. ""I will settle them in their homes" declares the Lord" (Hosea 11: 11b, NIV). There are children who need homes, a place of refuge in the physical. They are looking for a place of comfort and rest, and God seeks to hire you as the innkeeper to care after the hurt and bereaved. A psalmist describes it beautifully when he says, "God sets the lonely in families" (Psalm 68:6a, NIV). If we understand that God has the heart of the Samaritan, then read with me the next verse as if you were the innkeeper and God was the Samaritan speaking directly to you. Luke 10:35 (NIV) says, "The next day [the Samaritan] took out two denarii and gave them to the innkeeper. 'Look after him,' he said, 'and when I return, I will reimburse you for any extra expense you may have.'" God has given you your portion to begin your ministry of love. He has placed in your hands two denarii.

While researching the value of two denarii, I found that because of the rapid change in inflation in the Roman Empire, the coin might have been valued almost nothing at one point and have great value at another. Just as the denarii then could represent a wide range of worth, so we as Christians have been given different amounts from the Lord. One thing holds true, we have been given something, and with that something we are subjected to the stewardship and multiplication of it. Some of you may have a comfortable lifestyle and others of you have time. Some of you have great wealth and still others wisdom or knowledge to endow others with in love. Then there is the vast amount of you who could have one or more of these in abundance if you looked at your assets carefully and consumed either your time or your money with scrutiny. In any regard, we all have our two denarii, and it lays in our hands. Our talents have been distributed, and God is gently asking you not to bury them.

The Father to the fatherless looks up at you and says 'Look after him, the orphan, after her, the widow, because I am returning for this broken one and for you. And when, not if, but when I come back I will repay you for everything that you poured out on my beloved. I will repay you for hardship and ridicule you endured, and for the finances, time, and mercy you poured in to my orphan, and for the times you had to go without financially, materially, and socially. This is because you sacrificed to do my will. But I need you to trust me; trust me that I am coming back and that I am bringing my reward with me.' The riches we will reap in heaven for looking after his children will far exceed the hardships we may endure in this lifetime. Altogether, it is because we endure in doing right that we will be rewarded. "But when you give a banquet, invite the poor, the crippled, the lame, the blind, and you will be blessed. Although they cannot repay you, you will be repaid at the resurrection of the righteous" (Luke 14:13-14, NIV).

This poise of thought is more than a lighthearted suggestion in God's word for attempted application in our present lives. It is highlighted in prophecy and told by the mouths of old voice pieces from God. Adoption as revealed in this book is surely not the final fulfillment of these words, but just as each scripture speaks to us personally day to day and is seen fulfilled in our intimate relationships and small constructed lives, there are also larger fulfillments of God's word before the greatest and final achievement takes place. When I passed by a captivating scripture in Isaiah, it engulfed my heart before I understood its full implication for this writing. Let us ponder it together. Isaiah 49:22-23a (NIV, 1984) reads:

> This is what the Sovereign LORD says:
> "See, I will beckon to the Gentiles,
> I will lift up my banner to the peoples;
> they will bring your sons in their arms
> and carry your daughters on their shoulders.
> Kings will be your foster fathers,
> and their queens your nursing mothers."

Here the Lord is talking to the Israelites. The seed of Abraham is the intended recipient of this word. God is speaking a hard word to the Israelites, telling them that other nations, in their minds eye – heathens, will bring them their children. How could the Gentiles bring the Israelites own children to the Israelites? It does not make any sense. Ah! But it does. The children of Israel are the children of Abraham. Remember that Israel is the new name given to Jacob who is the grandson in the lineup of Abraham, Isaac, and Jacob. We know that God said that Abraham would have children that would be as numerous as the stars in the sky, and those children are children of faith, not just of human bloodline. "In other words, it is not the children by physical descent who are God's children, but it is the children of the promise who are regarded as Abraham's offspring" (Romans 9:8, NIV). When Jesus came, He opened the door for all people everywhere to receive salvation. So the Gentiles will be bringing in not just the bloodline of Abraham but the 'faithline' of Abraham to the nation God so cherishes.

According to the next phrases, Gentiles will bring the sons of faith in their arms and will carry daughters of righteousness on their shoulders. If someone is going to carry anyone else, would it not be through material means? Would it not be through love and mercy? Would it not also look like the kindness of inviting a stranger into a home? This word is not something that God is begging anyone to do. He is, in fact, proclaiming that it is already done from the beginning. It is a truth the Lord will unfold and bring to manifest on earth.

God speaks of further detail into the situation. He describes the kind of people that will partake in this grandiose presentation of children. He says it will be kings and it will be queens that do this work of a servant. Interesting, isn't it? As I looked up those two words in the Hebrew, I saw adjectives such as 'noble' to describe the feminine term and 'royal' to describe the masculine. God has named some people as such. In fact, it is *us* He calls these things. In 1 Peter 2:9 we are referred to as a royal priesthood. The word royal from this verse means "kingly" in the Greek. The people called to carry these children are not just any Gentile but these are believing Gentiles. Many of us are not from Israeli descent, so we are Gentiles. What makes us trust worthy to carry the seed of Abraham on our shoulders is that we too are madly in love with God and unashamedly loyal to His name. What was obviously the most intriguing and stunning sign of this passage was the word "foster". From what I knew, foster was a term of modern times. How could it possibly be used in the bible? The feasibility is that it is a modern translation to a permanent idea of the original language.

In the New King James version, the term 'foster fathers' in the NIV is translated as 'nursing fathers'. Odd sounding that the fathers should nurse, don't you think? The clarification lies in the Hebrew. This term 'nursing fathers' is best understood in English by a culmination of two proper translations: 'to build up or support' and 'to foster as a parent or nurse'. Figuratively it illustrates rendering 'faithful', 'to be permanent'. How absolutely amazing! So the nursing father is just that. He is the one is building up his son or 'nursing' him from childhood into adulthood. The permanency factor means only one thing: that this is not the fostering that we think of today in America, where placement happens as randomly and as often as the wind blows. This is the concept of taking one into your home and accepting him or her as yours forever. Likewise, the term nursing mothers translates 'to suck' or to be the causing agent to give milk. Now we have the right gender! Just as young Christians when they are first born again must be given milk to understand the basic principles of Christianity, so too, these infants of love must be fed love from a mother who will cause them to receive it. These queens are nurturing a child in the faith and in the physical to a mature and complete person. Of course God ultimately is the one who feeds us. In these verses, God says Himself that He will "beckon" the Gentiles, us, to do it. God is raising us up to feed those who are overlooked and forgotten today.

I appeal to you to invest your own life in the things ahead, which God offered you as a heritage to His name. Pass on the life God offers to the next generation. Raise up a generation of believers who, if left unattended, would stand at the foot of the cross in awe and weep at the throne of their Savior until they got vision. It is our goal to raise up such a people. These souls could stand in the gap for the lost and lonely children of their next generation. Justice is calling, and the Lion of the tribe of Judah is roaring just as Hosea has said it. It's time to wake up to what could become God's generation.

I believe if we catch this vision, it will enable the multitudes in the next generation to catch the vision the Lord has for them. What an awe inspiring picture it would be to see that we abandoned no child to the waywardness of sin and desperation but took them all in our hands and held them up to the light of truth. We might live to see the generation that is blessed of the Lord. It will not be an easy feat; rather the forces against the move of God are strong and rampant. However, the Word of the Lord does more than just encourage us to do it; prophecy says we can because it declares this is destined to happen. Rise up with me men and women of faith, and fight with the weapons of love.

Epilogue

Back to Life

In April of 2011, I attended TheCall pre-rally in Dallas which would lead up to The Call: Back to Life in Dallas the following spring. This particular rally was focused on the ending of abortion and mercy for our nation. During one of the sessions, Lou Engle showed a short video made by CatholicVote.org. The video displayed clips of pro-choice, pro-Planned Parenthood rallies. The amount of anger and verbal abrasiveness was a bit more ruthless and brash than I expected. The people knew exactly what they stood against, and they had the slogans to prove it. I had never really seen a pro-choice rally and had never been exposed to the well-defined arguments of the other side.

As I watched the video, a couple of comments made by protesters were like darts to my spirit that shocked me. I began to get a better understanding at the perspective of the modern day pro-choice movement. One young woman said in a jeering fashion, "A baby's going to get in the way of a job that I need to get to pay off those loans." I suppose this comment feeds right back to the earlier study findings which said that money was the number one cause for abortion. Hearing these words from the lips of a real person and watching the attitude behind it was like studying a creature I had heard about but had never seen. The contempt in her voice was definitive. I think her contempt was meant to be aimed at the pro-life movement and the religious sect, but the truth is that her contempt was for life. She obviously valued the American dollar over a child.

A young college-aged male made this statement, "I want a Planned Parenthood to be like Starbucks. I want a Planned Parenthood on every corner." Crushing to the compassionate heart, this man valued his sex life over human life, just as many value their own promiscuous sexual habits. He wanted the reward of marriage without the natural consequences. The innocence he bore on his face did not match the abominable words that came out of his mouth. They revealed the evil of his personal life. For every woman he impregnated, he wanted an easy way out of his God-given responsibility as a man. This hedonistic approach, says that pleasure is a goal lofty enough to dispose life by murdering another. I take pity on these young people's hearts because they truly do not know what they are saying. There is a veil over their eyes, and they do not understand that life is not all about them and that God sees the unborn as beautiful and valuable. One lead protester shouted into a microphone, "There is no shame in abortion!" During the rally we prayed corporately for the demonstrators' eyes to be opened and their hearts to receive salvation. I pray even now for mercy to reign down on them, and for the Lord's love to revolutionize their desires.

As amazing of testimonies these words were to me, these were not the words that sent the final revelation stirring in me.

Something more powerful was said. These young people, though they didn't know it, were giving a strategy to end abortion. They thought it was the ridiculousness of the comment that argued for murder, but it was actually an answer against it. "They're all about saving the fetus, but they're not about raising the kid," said one young man. He is right. Until this point, the church has had staunch protestors, demonstrations, organizations, teachings, books, endless amounts of educational websites and pamphlets about the sin of abortion, but we didn't offer a solution. This young man gave the church a charge. What he was really saying was, "If you really believe in what you are standing for and you really want to fix this, then come fix it yourself! If you claim you are the church, then come be the church." The words echoed through my mind, and a new fire began to rise up inside me.

We cannot merely stand against something anymore like we have merely stood against abortion, we have to stand *for* something. Our branding is the pro-life movement, and if we are going to be about the fetus, then we need to be about raising the kid. I had heard it said so beautifully that we cannot hold the standards of Christ to people who are not Christians. They do not have the mind, which is their will, or the power, which is given by the Holy Spirit, to carry it out. We are asking the ungodly to live like the godly, and that is impossible. What we need to be doing is saving the ungodly and live like we are godly.

I don't know if it was by the God-ordained interference of the Holy Spirit upon the mouth of this one young girl, or just the thoughts of her reasoning for attending the rally that led her to this quote, but she presented the undeniable answer. "Unless you're going to start adopting all these kids that are going to be born, I don't know what we are going to do. We don't have the maintenance." What she said is exactly right. They don't have the maintenance because they are living in sin and like it, and they have no compelling power to help themselves in the situation that has been created. We have got to start being the answer. If Christ was the answer for us, then his love must be the answer for the world. Adoption is our answer.

The words of the pro-choice young adults in the video felt like a rolling wave that was coming at me. Their words built upon the ears of my heart. I could hear the voices telling me, 'Your all about the fetus.' "Abortion is health care." "There is no shame." "Keep your rosaries off my ovaries." "Unless you're going to start adopting . . . I don't know what we're going to do." However, a greater overcoming standard was rising inside of me, and God was giving me fresh words. The new mantra of the church should be, "We will take on your burden! We will receive your babies! We will accept your children!" I have a vision of adoption agencies standing alongside 5 or even 10 of their potential adoptive couples outside the front doors of abortion clinics as a sign to the pregnant mothers walking in. I want every abortion-minded mother to know that *we* will be her answer; death does not have to be. Mother Teresa has been assumed to these words stated so simply but with an intense punch of truthful compassion, "Abortion is murder in the womb...A child is a gift of God. If you do not want him, give him to me." I think the second sentence echoes into the depths of my spirit every time I hear it. Its reverberations stop time around me and astound my heart. "If you do not want him, give him to me." She seems to say, if you can't find value in your child, know that I already did. The words of Mother Teresa can be the words of our own mouths.

For every abortion protestor, book writer and book reader, for every pro-life organizer, donor, and event attendee there needs to be a willing adoptive family. If we are willing to talk the talk, then we must be willing to walk the walk. I believe that there will come a day very soon when it will be the norm for every Christian household in America to adopt at least one child in addition to their natural-born children. When Roe v. Wade is overturned, the one million legal abortions every year will turn into one million legal unwanted children. In addition, almost 200,000 children in the foster care system have terminated parental rights who desperately need a family to love them, and every year more children end up in that category. The American church has a calling to adopt one million plus children every year. If God is giving the burden, that does not mean it is easy, but it does mean that with God it is possible. I am calling you just as I hear God calling us to be the lovers of the forgotten and unwanted. This mantra must be lived out by faith. As Christians rise to be the representation of Jesus Christ in this God-ordained hour, we will reap a harvest of believers in this nation that will have the might, power, and influence, even by sheer number if they do not leave the faith, to tear down the walls of unrighteousness that has been building up for generations past. Then the standard of wickedness that arose to encumber us in our generation can be encumbered and defeated by the power of love and godliness in theirs, but that is another chapter yet to be written by your hand . . . The children are waiting.

Works Cited

All Greek/Hebrew translations are from E-Sword.

All Bible references in all translations are from www.biblegateway.com

Adomites, Paul and Saul Wisnia. <u>Babe Ruth</u>. "Babe Ruth Enters St. Mary's Industrial School for Boys". From: <u>The Babe Ruth Story</u> by Babe Ruth and Bob Considine. 1948. http://entertainment.howstuffworks.com/babe-ruth2.htm

Adoption Exchange Association. "About Adoption". How do I Adopt Children from Foster Care. 2 Sept 2010. http://www.adoptuskids.org/resourceCenter/about-adoption.aspx

Ann E. Casey Foundation. "Data Across States: Children in Single-Parent Family Homes." Kids Count Data Center. 2009. Retrieved 1 Jan 2011. http://datacenter.kidscount.org/data/acrossstates/Rankings.aspx?ind=106

Barbara Bush. General Quote. "Family Quotes to Ponder". Christian Parenting Source. http://www.christian-parenting-source.com/family-quotes.html

Blowland, S. <u>In the Shadow of Fame: A memoir by the daughter of Erik H. Erikson</u>. New York: Viking Press, 2005.

Bohlender, Randy. Teaching. Finding Adoption in the Prayer Movement. Forerunner Christian Fellowship.

Craig, Grace J., and Wendy L. Dunn. Understanding Human Development. Upper Saddle River: Pearson Prentice Hall, 2007.

Dobson, James. What Women wish their Husbands knew about Them. Wheaton: Tyndale House, 1975.

Engle, Lou. Nazarite DNA. Kansas City: The Call, Inc.

Engler, Barbara. Personality Theories: An Introduction. 3rd ed. Boston, Massachussetts: Houghton Mifflin Company, 1991.

Frost, Jack and Trisha. "From Slavery to Sonship (1-2)". Shiloh Place Ministries. http://www.shilohplace.org/resources

Haim, Ginott. The December List. "Quotations". http://unixmama.com/december/quotes.html

Hennessy, Jim. No More Cotton Candy, Energizing Your Spiritual Life with More of God's Presence and Power. Springfield: Onward Books, 2011.

Jim Hennessy, Senior Pastor. Sermon "Mandate for Manhood". Trinity Church of Cedar Hill. 2011.

Joshua Project. "Great Commission Statistics". http://www.joshuaproject.net/great-commission-statistics.php

Kendall, Diana. Social Problems in a Diverse Society. 4th ed. Boston: Pearson, 2007.

James, Teddy. "Adoption – a profound picture of the Gospel." American Family Association Journal May 2011: 10-12. Print.

Jacobs, Cindy. The Reformation Manifesto. Minneapolis: Bethany House, 2008.

Lincoln, Abraham. General Quote. "The December List". http://unixmama.com/december/quotes.html

Lou Engle. Speaker. "The Doctrine of the Shedding of Innocent Blood." Austin, TX. 2010.

Miller, Mona and Gina Russo. Pew Trusts. "Report Finds 41% Jump in Teens 'Aging Out' of Foster Care". News Room Detail. 2 Sept 2010. http://www.pewtrusts.org/news_room_detail.aspx?id=26136

Merriam-Webster. http://www.merriam-webster.com

Mother Teresa. All Great Quotes. http://www.allgreatquotes.com/mother_teresa_quotes.shtml

Nathanson, Bernard. "The Silent Scream." American Portrait Films. (1984 Documentary) 8 Apr 2008. <http://youtube.com/watch?v=cjNo_0cW-ek>

National Rights to Life Educational Trust Fund. "Abortion Statistics: United States Data and Trends". 2011. http://www.nrlc.org/factsheets/fs03_abortionintheus.pdf

Neufeldt, Victoria, ed, et al. Webster's New World College Dictionary. 3rd ed. New York: Macmillan, 1997.

Nordeman, Nicole. "Small Enough." This Mystery. Sparrow Records. 2000.

O'Hare, William P. "Data on Children in Foster Care from the Census Bureau". The Annie E. Casey Foundation. June 2008. 2 Sept 2010. http://www.aecf.org/~/media/PublicationFiles/FosterChildrenJuly2508.pdf

Ortiz-Portillo, Elena. "Mental Health Aspects of Miscarraige and Induced Abortion." Psychiatric Times 23.3 (March 1, 2006): 48. InfoTrac Psychology Collection. Gale. Dallas Baptist University. 8 Apr 2008 <http://find.galegroup.com/itx/start.do?prodId=SPJ.SP09>

PBS. "Orphan Trains". American Experience. http://www.pbs.org/wgbh/amex/orphan/

Quintana, Chris. "Father-son duo publish book as blog and podcast." The New Mexican on the Web 02 Aug. 2012. http://www.santafenewmexican.com/Local%20News/071512Lovatos

Robertson, Pat. The Ten Offenses: Reclaim The Blessings of The Ten Commandments. Nashville: Integrity, 2004.

Santelli, John S., et al. "An Exploration of the Dimensions of Pregnancy Intentions Among Women Choosing to Terminate Pregnancy or to Initiate Prenatal Care in New Orleans, Louisiana." American Journal of Public Health 96.11 (November 2006) 2009-2015. InfoTrac Psychology Collection. Gale. Dallas Baptist University. 8 Apr 2008. <http://find.galegroup.com/itx/start.do?prodId=SPJ.SP09>

Schultz, Duane P., and Sydney Ellen Schultz. Theories of Personality. 9th ed. Belmont: Wadsworth Cengage Learning, 2009.

Siegel, Larry J., and Brandon C. Welsh. Juvenile Delinquency: The Core. 3rd ed. Belmont: Thompson Wadsworth, 2008.

Steve Robinson, Senior Pastor. Sermon. Church of the King. Mandeville, Louisiana. 2009.

Stringer, Doug. Who's Your Daddy Now?. Cheshire: GateKeeper Publishing, 2007.

Swindoll, Charles R. Elijah: A Man of Heroism and Humility. Nashville: W Publishing Group, 2000.

Taylor, Justin. The Gospel Coalition. "Number of Abortions Since 1973". 2009 http://thegospelcoalition.org/blogs/justintaylor/2009/01/03/number-of-abortions-since-1973/

The Pew Charitable Trusts. "Time for Reform: Aging Out and on Their Own (More teens leaving foster care without a permanent family). 2007. 2 Sept 2010. http://www.pewtrusts.org/uploadedFiles/wwwpewtrustsorg/Reports/Foster care reform/Kids are Waiting Timefor Reform0307.pdf

U.S. Bureau of Labor Statistics, updated and revised from "Families and Work in Transition in 12 Countries, 1980-2001," Monthly Labor Review, September 2003, with national sources, some of which may be unpublished. Internet release date: 9/30/2011. 1 Jan 2011. http://www.bls.gov/opub/mlr/mlrhome.htm

United States. U.S. Department of Health and Human Services. Administration for Children and Families. Administration on Children, Youth, and Families. Children's Bureau. <u>The AFCARS (Adoption and Foster Care Analysis and Reporting System) Report FY 2009</u>. Washington: GPO?, 2010

---. ---. ---. ---. ---. "Trends in Foster Care and Adoption". Statistics and Research. 2 Sept 2010. <u>http://www.acf.hhs.gov/programs/cb/stats_research/afcars/trends.htm</u>

---. ---. ---. ---. ---. "Children in Public Foster Care Waiting to be Adopted: FY 1999 thru FY 2006". 2 Sept 2010. <u>http://www.acf.hhs.gov/programs/cb/stats_research/afcars/adoptchild06.pdf</u> (?)

University of Oregon. "Fostering and Foster Care". The Adoption History Project. <u>http://www.uoregon.edu/~adoption/topics/fostering.htm</u>

Upton, Jason. "Father of the Fatherless." <u>Between Earth and Sky</u>. Key of David Ministries. 2007.

"Youth & Labor". United States Department of Labor. <u>http://www.dol.gov/dol/topic/youthlabor/index.htm</u>